Fighting Truth Decay!

Fighting Truth Decay!

the message of Jude

Sam Gordon

AMBASSADOR

BELFAST, NORTHERN IRELAND
GREENVILLE, SOUTH CAROLINA

FIGHTING TRUTH DECAY
© 2002 Trans World Radio

All Scripture quotations, unless indicated, are taken from the *Holy Bible: New International Version*. Copyright © 1973, 1978, 1984, International Bible Society. All rights reserved.

ISBN 1 84030 121 X

Ambassador Publications
a division of
Ambassador Productions Ltd.
Providence House
Ardenlee Street
BELFAST
BT6 8QJ
Northern Ireland
www.ambassador-productions.com

Emerald House
427 Wade Hampton Blvd.
GREENVILLE
SC 29609, USA
www.emeraldhouse.com

Trans World Radio
11 St James Gardens
SWANSEA
SA1 6DY
United Kingdom

01792 483050

www.twr.org.uk

Trans World Radio
P O Box 8700
CARY
NC 27512, USA

1 800 456 7TWR

www.twr.org

DEDICATION

to

David and Joan Lamkin

with admiration, appreciation, and affection

Truth for Today

~ Mission Statement ~

'To teach the entire Bible in a warm expository style so that people's lives are influenced to such a degree that they impact their world for Christ.'

Books in the **Truth for Today** series:

REVELATION:
Worthy is the Lamb

1 - 2 - 3 JOHN:
Living in the Light

JUDE:
Fighting Truth Decay

First Word

Where you lived didn't matter. How wealthy you were didn't matter. Who you were didn't matter. September 11, 2001 was a date we will all remember. When those hijacked airplanes were flown into the twin towers of the World Trade Center in New York, into the Pentagon in Washington DC, and into the ground in Western Pennsylvania, civilised people around the world were horrified. As an American, I was especially saddened when I watched those twin wonders of architecture crumble to the ground, knowing they were filled with people, many of whom would not know the Lord. The scene is indelibly impressed into my mind.

But there was another tragedy that day. It didn't dominate the news for the next week or ten days. In fact, it didn't make the news at all. This tragedy reveals more of the inadequacy of the Christian heart than the hatred of the radical Muslim heart. The tragedy of which I speak was the almost total inability of Christians to give adequate, biblical answers to questions about how this could happen. And not just American Christians; Christians everywhere were curiously at a loss for a 'biblical perspective' on the tragedies. Why?

Truth decay!

We have become so unfamiliar with God's word in good times that we are often unable to summon its strength in bad times. Truth has become so twisted in the world. Not much makes sense anymore. But this is not new to the third millennium; it was true in the first century as well. The tiny epistle of Jude bears witness to that.

Sam Gordon has become well known as a Bible expositor who cuts to the chase, and this work, *Fighting Truth Decay*, is no exception. With skill and care, Sam takes us on a journey through the twenty-five short verses of this powerful letter. He highlights the truth twisters that Jude faced, many of whose descendants we face today. He counsels us how to keep our distance from grumblers, nit pickers, big heads, and church splitters. Through this delightful study of a delightful New Testament book, Sam Gordon helps us keep both our wits and our focus while we learn to keep company with God and godly people.

While the epistle of Jude hits head-on the troublesome topic of those who would twist the truth and rob us of answers when we need them most, Sam says, 'Jude preferred to accentuate the positive rather than emphasise the negative'. That's what he does as well. Any commentary on a book such as Jude could easily turn out to be a 'thou shalt not' commentary. This one doesn't. Oh, to be sure, there are cautions to be found here, but in dealing with those who would contaminate us and rob us of biblical truth, Sam Gordon is careful to balance caution with confidence in our victory in Christ.

'The best way to protect ourselves against false teaching is to familiarise ourselves with the truth of Scripture,' says the author. Had we heeded that advice prior to September 11, perhaps we would have been better comforters in tragedy, better counsellors when faced with uncertainty, better Christians when we needed to be.

You will enjoy your journey through Jude with Sam Gordon as your guide. He is faithful to the text, forthright in his exposure of those who cause truth decay, and fervent in his defence of the true faith. Once you take this journey you will be prompted to find God's answers to man's problems so that, should you be on the front line of tragedy, you will speak the truth in love, without fear of truth decay.

Dr Woodrow Kroll

President
Back to the Bible International

Summer 2002

Second Thoughts

1985 was a memorable year for me. That was the year Dr Sam Lowry of Ambassador Publications chose to publish my first ever book, *Jewels from Jude*.

The response from all around the world to that easy read, verse-by-verse commentary exceeded our wildest dreams and expectations. Down through the years, I have met many folk who were richly blessed and helped through it. At the same time, I have heard of many preachers who have also used it with great profit.

Such stories of changed lives never fail to thrill and gladden my heart. It is a humbling experience when that happens and I am more than happy to give my Lord and Saviour all the glory.

In recent years there has been a growing demand for *Jewels from Jude* to be reprinted. Up until a few months ago, however, that project had been left to simmer on the back burner. Now, I am pleased to say, in the summer of 2002, seventeen years and twelve books later, it has reappeared.

In fact, there is no comparison between this volume and its earlier edition. Apart from a new title and a fresh format, the contents have largely been rewritten. There is also a superb study guide appended to the text which makes it ideal for personal and group use.

If you already own a copy of *Jewels from Jude*, you can purchase *Fighting Truth Decay* with total confidence. In every sense, this is a brand new book, one you cannot afford to be without!

Sam Gordon

Contents

1

The patron saint of lost causes

Believe it or not, there *is* a book called Jude in the New Testament! It is not the last book in the Bible, by any means. It is the last, but one!

That means Jude is the penultimate epistle in the extensive library of the Word of God. Sixty-six books in total and Jude comes in at number 65! It immediately precedes the awesome, Jesus-on-every-page book of Revelation and it proceeds directly after the brief Post-it note of 3 John.

Jude is sandwiched neatly between two Johannine bookends. On his left, we have a warm endearing letter to a marvellous friend called Gaius; on his right, we have a fasten-your-seatbelt, hold-your-breath panorama of cosmic events which herald the climax of the ages as they unfold in the Apocalypse.

Jude is only a single chapter occupying not more than a couple of pages in the average size Bible. It comprises 25 verses in total and can be easily read within four or five minutes. Do not under-estimate our friend Jude! Even though he may be little, he has an awful lot to say. Jude is not given to verbosity, that is true, but he has an uncanny knack of making every word count. Jude knows where he is going. And he gets there!

His message is unbelievably powerful. It is extremely potent. We can look at it like this:

- think of a tiny dose of penicillin which can heal a person of a deadly disease,

- think of a small handheld personal computer which can carry vast amounts of vital information,
- think of the mighty Goliath of Gath, felled with one little stone.

Well, that is what Jude can do!

In the gracious providence of God, this diminutive letter can heal sick and ailing churches, it can inform and clarify the thinking of God's people at a significant time in world history, it can slay giant threats to the spiritual lives of well-meaning Christians.

Jude's analysis of the prevailing winds of church life is so perceptive and clear, and his recommendations so razor sharp, that the letter has a finer cutting edge and contemporary feel than we might initially think. I believe the book of Jude scratches where people are itching. It gives answers to the questions that ordinary people are asking. It packs a punchy and persuasive message to Christians living in a world of replicas and counterfeits. It deals with what it really means to be a Christian in word and deed, and helps us to be nothing less in our time.

The undeniable fact that Jude is relegated to the sidelines by the average Christian is quite unfortunate. Such folk read the first few verses in his book and, it has to be said, because they are not overly impressed and because it does not warm the cockles of their heart, they quickly flick back to something more palatable and uplifting. To me, that is a terrible shame for Jude does not deserve that kind of treatment.

Traditionally, Jude is known as the patron saint of lost causes and sometimes, when it seems as though we are hitting our head against a brick wall, the gospel itself can seem like a lost cause. However, it seems to me, this obscurity and criticism is unwarranted, unjustified, and uncalled for.

The key question is: why is it so important for the church in the third millennium to study the book of Jude? Just as the book of Acts describes the halcyon days at the beginning of the church age, so Jude describes the tough, grit-your-teeth days at the end of the church age. Since Acts has been referred to as the Acts of the Apostles, S. Maxwell Coder has suggested that Jude could well be named the 'Acts of the Apostates!'

Three thousand years ago, King David raised the stakes when he asked in Psalm 11:3 this probing question: 'When the foundations are being destroyed, what can the righteous do?'

I am sure you will agree with my assessment when I say that we live in a day when biblical truth is opposed both outside and inside the so-called evangelical church. However, this is where the book of Jude finds its particular niche. It comes into play for it addresses that critical issue, and a host of others, head-on.

Can you honestly remember the last time you listened to a sermon preached from the book of Jude? When was the last occasion your daily reading manual touched upon Jude? Have you ever picked up a commentary on Jude as you have browsed through the well-laden shelves of your favourite Christian bookshop? The chances are, the answer to all three questions is negative.

Assuming that is the case, permit me to introduce you to the man and his message.

When did Jude write his epistle?

'I wish I knew!' is the simple straightforward answer. It is a bit like the Heinz phenomenon for there are 57 answers to that one six million dollar question. The reality is, no-one knows for sure. We can only assume and presume as we tentatively read between the lines. In other words, we cannot be dogmatic on this one!

Having said that, it was obviously penned during the rapid rise of Gnosticism, a fashionable and trendy pre-Christian philosophy. That much is unmistakably clear from the inferences in the book itself. Gnostics saw Christianity as having distinct advantages and what they did was to incorporate the bits they liked into their system. Adolf Harnack defined Gnosticism as the 'acute secularising of Christianity'.

These folk saw themselves in the premier league; to them, everyone else was in the lower divisions when it came to matters of faith. They felt they were superior and, consequently, lived on a different level to ordinary Christian people. They marketed themselves as a kind of super-spiritual elitist company. In their eyes, they were in a class of their own.

Another factor to take into consideration is that the Faith was slowly but surely being corrupted by impostors. The words of warning from the apostles have had ample time to do the rounds and are now proving to be true. The fact that Jude refers to what the apostles said rather than wrote would seem to suggest that we are still moving within the oral period. Those were the days when apostolic teaching was passed on by word of mouth.

Drawing the various strands together, it would lend itself to the view that Jude put quill to parchment during the early years of the second half of the first century.

First impressions

It is really quite incredible, given the jaundiced prejudice of some, that the vast majority of the early church fathers had little or no difficulty in recognising the authenticity of Jude's epistle.

It finds a place in the second century Muratorian Canon (AD 170). We know that Tertullian of North Africa (AD 160-225) viewed it as an authoritative Christian document. So did Clement of Alexandria (AD 150-215) who actually wrote a commentary on it. Origen (AD 185-254), biblical scholar and prolific writer, hints in his writings that there were serious doubts in his day, but clearly he did not share them.

To Origen, the book of Jude is *'an epistle filled with flowing words of heavenly grace.'*

The noted Christian apologist, Athenagoras of Athens, together with Polycarp (AD 69-155), later martyred as Bishop of Smyrna, and Barnabas, seem to have cited the epistle early in the second century. By the time the year AD 200 had dawned, the epistle of Jude was freely accepted in the three main areas of the ancient church: Alexandria, Rome, and Africa. The Italian biblical scholar, Jerome (AD 347-419), author of the Vulgate Bible (the first Latin translation of the Bible from the Hebrew) also acknowledged it as a genuine article. Some time later it was confirmed as a Holy Spirit inspired piece of literature whose human author was Jude when it was recognised in the canon at the Third Council of Carthage in AD 397.

Who is on the receiving end?

Again, like the dating of the letter, we have no clear indication as to the recipients of this timely note. For starters, we do not know whether they were specifically of Gentile origin or if they were of Jewish extraction. It is fairly obvious from verses 3-5 that their exact and precise geographical location is also shrouded in a cloak of mystery.

Jude himself is a Jew and that colours his thinking and taints his theology.

The inspired writer assumes their knowledge of inter-testamental and apocryphal literature. He takes it for granted that they are familiar with what was written during the four hundred silent years between the end of Malachi and the beginning of Matthew.

Over and over again, Jude makes reference to happenings recorded on the pages of the Old Testament; that much is clear from what he says in verse 11 where he mentions the infamously egregious and egoistic trio of Cain, Balaam, and Korah.

One commentator hits the nail on the head when he concludes: *'The references are such that only a Jew could understand them, and its allusions are such that only a Jew could catch them.'*

When we stop and think about it, he is probably right!

What is different about Jude?

It appears to me, within the confines of the New Testament, Jude is quite unique. He quotes freely and fully from Jewish apocryphal literature. I realise that sometimes this jars in the minds of evangelical Christians. It is a practice that many find a little too hot to handle.

Let me give you a handful of examples: the information in verse 9 is gleaned from the Assumption of Moses, whereas the gist of what is enshrined in verses 14 and 15 is documented from the book of Enoch. These books were probably written some time during the second or first century before Christ and were freely in circulation among the Jewish communities of New Testament times. Jude may also have been referring to the Testament of Naphtali in verse 6 and to the Testament of Asher in verse 8.

The fact is, there is nothing wrong with that! It is like the modern preacher quoting from the works of Rudyard Kipling or John Bunyan or, perhaps, a contemporary song by Graham Kendrick.

A high view of the doctrine of biblical inspiration does not preclude the writer's privilege to quote at random from outside sources.

Christopher Green keeps the matter in perspective when he suggests that 'Jude's quotations mean neither that we should include his sources in our Bibles nor that we should exclude his letter from our Bibles.'

The bottom line is that Jude is answering the claims of the false teachers from their own preferred material. They extract the deliciously juicy bits they want and leave the rest, but Jude goes to the same literature, and hits them between the eyes with it. That is, Jude plays them, and beats them, at their own game!

Jude can find an able ally in the apostle Paul who selected relevant data from extra-biblical Jewish writings in 1 Corinthians 15:33 and again in 2 Timothy 3:8 where he referred to Jannes and Jambres in their opposition to Moses. Paul even culled some illustrative material from the heathen poets in his famous and memorable sermon on the Areopagus at Athens as recorded in Acts 17:28. He does the same thing in his pastoral letter to Titus where he says, 'Even one of their own prophets has said, "Cretans are always liars, evil brutes and lazy gluttons"' (Titus 1:12).

I firmly believe when we pick up the little book of Jude in our hand that we are holding the word of God. And because it is the living word of the living God, it demands our total obedience and it deserves our whole-hearted allegiance.

Fighting truth decay?

That poser is both obvious and inevitable and it is one that deserves a straight answer. No ground is gained by being evasive. How can we justify Jude's comments? He is, as it were, making a contrast between truth and error. He writes to combat this influx of heresy which he sees overwhelming and endangering the people of God.

Jude, however, is no mere polemicist, spoiling for a fight, seeking any excuse for controversy. As Christopher Green points out, 'He too has a pastor's heart. Jude's ambition is not only to pull down the strongholds of error, but to see that the loyal believers build up one another in Christ.'

The most important feature of this heresy is that it constitutes a concerted twin-pronged attack on the moral purity of the church and the doctrinal truth about Jesus Christ. According to Jude in verse 4, these heretics *'change the grace of God into a licence for immorality and deny Jesus Christ our only Sovereign and Lord'.* The fact is, perversion of the gospel leads to perversion of Christian morality.

Before we go any further, it is worth noting that Jude's attitude is clearly out of step with that of today's world and its dominant mindset. Jude's passionate concern for truth is often viewed in our day as something which is out of date and behind-the-times. It is looked on as a kind of anachronism.

The tragedy is that today's generation is in the process of throwing the baby out with the bath water.

By and large, these folk want to abandon the notion of objective truth, especially in matters of faith and spirituality. We hear a lot today in certain sections of the media about post-modernism and the New Age movement. Whether we like it or not, they are impacting our world more than we realise; if the truth be told, they are shaping the culture of the third millennium. Basically, when all is cut and dried, they are two sides of the same coin.

The New Age movement tells people they have the power inside them to shape their own reality. Post-modernism tells people that reality is only what they subjectively perceive it to be.

No matter what way you look at it, from that perspective, truth is a fluid commodity. It is something which is malleable in the hands of human beings. Truth is what you and I want it to be. It is relative and, therefore, it appeals to the existentialist mindset.

We also hear a lot about globalisation; that theme is currently riding high on the world agenda. The movers and shakers in our day espouse it and hold it close to their hearts. The spirit of our times informs me that we live in a multi-faith society, a pluralistic society, a society which insists that no one religion can claim to have a monopoly on the truth. For the sake of peace and because he does not want to rock the boat, the man on the street is happy to treat every opinion as an equally valid opinion. In other words, one man's view is as credible as the next man's! Tolerance is the word that springs to mind.

I am afraid Jude's statement in verse 4, which I quoted a moment ago, does not sit easily with the spirit of our age. 'All faiths lead to God' is a slogan which Jude definitely does not subscribe to.

For the committed believer with an authentic faith, the issue of truth is absolutely crucial.

There is so much at stake here. If contemporary society is right when it tells us there is no such a thing as 'truth' and that all paths lead to God, then, to put it bluntly, the Lord Jesus was wrong. It has to be one or the other, we cannot have it both ways!

This is not a matter of secondary importance or minor significance to the evangelical church. It is a matter of momentous proportions. We can see what is happening! Jude is seeking to establish clear lines of demarcation between the real and the spurious. He is focusing attention on the glaring difference between those who are genuine and those who are synthetic. People in the latter mould have an artificial faith which will neither stand the test of time or eternity.

Having deliberately forsaken that which is true, they have embraced in a willy-nilly fashion that which is false. Apostasy is the name of the game they are playing. Having boxed themselves into that corner, they are, in the purest sense of the word, apostates.

Jude's challenging letter shows they were making their presence felt in many local assemblies of God's people. They were dressed up in another gospel garb as they infiltrated one church after another. They claimed to be someone or something which they were not. At the end of the day, they were impostors.

Their brand of Christianity is theoretical. It is all in the mind, it has never touched or transformed the heart.

They are theological encyclopaedias on two legs! They know the truth from A to Z, but neither live by it or act upon it. They are phoney preachers and bogus believers. They are 'cosmetic' Christians.

That adds a new dimension, doesn't it. The English word comes from the Greek word *kosmetikos* which means 'a decorating or covering over'. It is to dress up something to give it an appearance on the surface that it lacks in reality. It looks good and it feels good, but it ain't good!

In other words, their religion is skin deep, it is merely superficial.

It seems to me that an apostate is someone who has received a measure of light but not life. He may have partaken to some degree of the written word, but he has not welcomed the living Word into his life.

Good soil, good soul

A superb illustration of this is found in the well-known parable of the sower. In that story, our Lord revealed that there is a class of men who are likened to seed sown on rocky ground. He says, 'they receive the word with joy when they hear it, but they have no root; they believe for a while, but in time of testing they fall away' (Luke 8:13).

The phrase 'fall away' chosen by Luke is the verb form of apostasy. Now, when we put it all together, this means that an apostate is one who receives the word, believes it for a time, then drifts away.

How can this be? Well, one possible explanation lies in the careful choice of language used by the Holy Spirit in the compiling of the accounts of this parable in the synoptic gospels. Although stony ground hearers are said to 'receive' the word, a much stronger term in the Greek is used of the good ground hearers. It is the word *paradechomai* as recorded in Mark 4:20.

You see, in direct contrast with the others, the good ground hearers 'receive to the side' the word of the Lord by welcoming it gladly into their hearts. Those who fall away are not said to understand the word, nor do they bring forth fruit. We see that reflected in Matthew 13:23. Ironically, they do not even have roots. Jude later draws upon this horticultural analogy in verse 12 when he says apostates are *'without fruit and uprooted, twice dead.'*

There is no point in us raising our eyebrows, shrugging our shoulders, and saying, 'that was then'. I can assure you, this is not a phenomenon restricted and confined to the past. It was not a seven day wonder in the first century of the primitive Christian movement. No, no, a thousand times no!

It is bang up-to-date.

The apostate files

The fact is, the word of Jude is a clarion call to the slumbering church of the twenty-first century to rouse herself. We need to wake up! Having wiped the sleep from our eyes, we need to get up and do something positive about it.

Satan is on the loose. The devil is on the run. Our adversary knows his days are numbered, he knows his time is short. As an angel of light, his strategy in these last days is to attack the church from within. Given time, he will do all in his power to rob the church of her life and heart.

The sad fact is, there are many organisations and denominations that litter the highway which once were pulsating with life. Today, they are dead or dying. They were vibrant. Now their bones rattle and vibrate on the graveyard of Christendom.

What has brought about the radical change in their fortunes? Generally speaking, they did not buckle under pressure from outside. It was not the heel of external oppression and opposition that caused them to crumble and crash. No, it came from within! It was the internal and infernal foe.

That is why Jude's timely letter is a warning to all of us to beware. We see what makes a real believer tick. But we also discover how a synthetic saint goes about his business of seriously undermining the work of God.

'Apostasy is an inside job, that is why it is so dangerous.' (Anon.)

2

Keeping it in the family

'Jude, a servant of Jesus Christ and a brother of James...'

verse 1a

A French taxicab driver picked up a passenger and safely delivered him to his plush five star hotel. On receiving payment and a generous tip, he said, *'Thank you, Sir Arthur Conan Doyle.'*

Sir Arthur, looking rather bemused, enquired, *'How did you know me?'*

He replied, *'I read in the newspaper that the famous author of the English detective Sherlock Holmes was coming to Paris from the South of France. I deduced from the cut of your clothes that you were English; observing your haircut and tanned face I knew that I could make a calculated guess.'*

'That is quite remarkable,' said Sir Arthur, *'And, please tell me, did you have any other evidence?'*

The driver said, *'Well, there is the label on your luggage!'*

The name on the label says it all!

The book begins with a single word, *'Jude'*. That just happens to be the signature of the man who penned the letter. I must confess, I am quite intrigued with his introduction. He tells us who he is right at the outset. Nothing more. Nothing else. Just Jude.

That shows me something of the plain humility of the man. His is an attractive modesty. There are no humbug airs or polished graces with this man, no lofty titles or highfalutin appellations. It does not matter where we meet him, he is always the same, he is his usual winsome self. There is nothing hoity-toity or la-di-da about him. There is nothing pompous or pretentious about him either. In computer-speak, when we look at Jude, what we see is what we get!

There is no indication of a holier-than-thou attitude being adopted by Jude. Nor is he pushy and bumptious about his particular brand of Christianity. As a preacher-man, he is down to earth. He radiates the gospel as he shines for Jesus in the midst of an inky black environment. Jude is a man who lived an authentic life in a world of cheap distortions.

But, oh, what a name!

It seems a terrible shame that someone so nice and affable should be handicapped with such an unfortunate choice of name.

Nevertheless, Jude is not responsible for what his parents inflicted on him. Isn't it wonderful though how God takes it and uses it to speak volumes to many needy hearts.

The cringe factor

In the original Greek this name is Judas. I am sure that name rings a bell with all of us! It is a name synonymous with betrayal. The name has been anathema since the early years of the first century when Judas engaged in an act of perfidious treachery and sold the Lord Jesus for thirty pieces of silver, the price of a common slave.

He was a traitor. Big time! He became the worst apostate the world has ever known. Now, in the providence of God, this single word ushers in a lone chapter devoted to the subject of apostasy within the professing church during the last days.

The plot begins to thicken, however, when we try to sort out which Judas we are thinking about. There are no fewer than five men of that name mentioned on the pages of the New Testament.

- Number one is the *Judas of Damascus* in whose home Paul was praying after his miraculous life changing conversion to faith in Jesus. We read about him in Acts 9:11.
- Number two is *Judas Barsabbas*, a leading light in the councils of the early church. He was alongside Silas when they conveyed the message to the church at Antioch concerning the decision of the Jerusalem

4

Council to throw open their doors to the Gentiles. He was also recognised as a prophet and that is intimated in a number of verses in Acts 15.

- Number three is the notorious *Judas Iscariot*. He was described by Jesus in John 17:12 as 'the son of perdition'. Here was a man with a promising start and, because of what he did, a predictably tragic end. He snuffed out his life by committing suicide.

I think none of these three names has ever seriously been considered as likely contenders for the authorship of this punchy letter. So, we will follow the tradition of our fathers and, likewise, rule them out. That leaves two more candidates for our screening and vetting process.

Three down, two to go

- Number four tells us there was a second Judas within the ranks of the apostolic band. He is carefully distinguished by John in his gospel as '*Judas ... not Judas Iscariot*' (John 14:22). In Luke's compilation of the Twelve there is an apostle whom the record refers to as 'Judas son of James' (*cf.* Luke 6:16, Acts 1:13). The three listings are speaking about the same individual. This Judas, then, was the son of a man named James, not his brother. This, therefore, cancels out his possible eligibility. There is only one left.
- Number five is the Judas who was the half-brother of Jesus. We read about him in Matthew 13:55 and Mark 6:3. At the same time, he could truly be called '*the brother of James*' because he was also one of our Lord's half-brothers.

It is interesting to note that James was often referred to as 'James the Righteous' or 'James the Just'. He probably wrote the New Testament letter that bears that name; as it happened, he was also a leading light in the Council of Jerusalem (*cf.* Acts 15:13-21). Actually, when push comes to shove, there is only one person in the early church whom everyone would know as 'James' without any ambiguity, and that was James the brother of Jesus (*cf.* Galatians 1:19).

S. Maxwell Coder astutely observed that James '*wrote his epistle to inform us of the need and importance of good works and that Jude wrote his letter to advise us of the danger of evil works.*'

Joseph and Simon were the remaining two male members of the Lord's earthly family. We know from the verses mentioned already that there were sisters in the family as well. The Greek word used for these half-brothers and half-sisters of Jesus is *adelphos* which means 'coming from the same womb'. These were children born to Mary and Joseph after Jesus was born. They were his half-brothers and half-sisters because Jesus was virgin born. In other words, they had the same mother but not the same father.

The day the penny dropped

I think it is perfectly reasonable to assume that Jude's conversion to faith in Christ must have taken place between the crucifixion and the ascension of his elder brother from the mount of Olives. We read in Acts 1:14 that after the Lord Jesus had risen and ascended into heaven that members of his family gathered for prayer with the disciples of Christ. That reference specifically includes the brothers of Jesus.

And so, by process of elimination, we have unravelled the mystery of his identification.

I think when we reflect on these close family ties we can see so much to cheer us and stimulate us to keep on praying for our loved ones who, as yet, do not know Jesus as Lord and Saviour. We all have family members (and friends) for whom we have been interceding for years, we have witnessed to them, we have tried to live the Christian life before them, and, apparently, it has all fallen on deaf ears.

Sometimes we feel as if we have really blown it and we end up on a long guilt trip. But, our friends, Jude and James, prove that God works in his own way and in his own time!

After all, these two lived in the same wee house as Jesus, they grew up alongside him, they played games with him in the street; in spite of that enormous privilege, they were unconverted for many years!

Even though the Lord turned the water into wine at the family wedding at Cana of Galilee, even though he healed the sick and fed the hungry thousands, even though he performed all kinds of miracles, none of this moved Jude, he appeared untouched and totally disinterested.

Somehow, with the best will in the world, he explained it all away, he rationalised his behaviour, there was no way he was going to go the way of Jesus, that was the last thing on his mind. But, we all know, the day came when Jude was converted.

Eventually ...

* ... the penny dropped!
* ... the evidence of the life of Jesus did begin to weigh with him, it slowly but surely began to make sense.
* ... God did work in his life through the family crisis of Jesus' death and the marvellous miracle of his resurrection.

It finally clicked! The light shone through! And that was that!

Take heart!

So, take heart! If your family seems to be doing all the wrong things, if they are sending you mixed signals, if they appear to be going on heedless and careless, do not give up, do not give in, keep on praying, keep on trusting. What God did for Jude, he can do for them!

It is good to remind ourselves, it was into this very ordinary family that the Lord Jesus was pleased to be born as a great sign of his solidarity with sinners like ourselves. It underlines the splendidly glorious truth that God loves sinners. It sounds infinitely better when we personalise it for it means, he loves you and me!

Yes, with a name like Jude, most people would run a mile or two, or three. Some of them might even be tempted to visit the local registrar, pay the appropriate fee, and change their name by deed poll.

But this one is different. He is perfectly content to see himself in verse one as *'a servant of Jesus Christ'*. It is a word that other New Testament Christians use of themselves and of one another. It has an overtone of great importance for Old Testament heroes like Abraham, Moses, David, and Daniel are all called 'servants of God'. It seems to me, Jude is moving in illustrious company.

The man with the pierced ear

The Greek word is *doulos* and it means Jude saw himself as a bondslave. This particular concept is found in the Old Testament book of Exodus. Upon his release from bondage, there were certain options available to the well-satisfied slave. According to Exodus 21, he could either leave his master or he could take advantage of staying with him as a bondslave. The principle is clear because here was a union based on love for, and loyalty to, his owner.

When the decision to remain was made, a strange ritual had to be observed. His ear would be bored through or pierced at the doorpost typifying his dedication to the slavery of love for evermore.

- The sprinkled blood on the doorpost when the ear was pierced declared, *'I believe'* (Exodus 12:23),
- the bored ear at the doorpost declared, *'I love'* (Deuteronomy 15:17),
- and the commandments written on the doorpost declared, *'I obey'* (Deuteronomy 6:9).

From this point on, the slave was committed irrevocably to his master. There was no turning back!

From Jude's perspective, that is the way it was! All day, every day, he was at his master's disposal, he was willing and eager to do whatever his master commanded. Whatever he did, he did out of a profound sense of loyalty and love. Jude was saying he is one who wears the chains of love, one who has found his liberty in becoming a slave to Christ.

I own no other master,
My heart shall be thy throne,
My life I give, henceforth to live,
O Christ, for thee alone.

A servant, not a star

It has to be said, so far as we can ascertain, Jude never used his fraternal relationship with Christ to impress other people. Genetics mean nothing when it comes to the kingdom of God.

Jude knows if he had laboured the point that he was from the same family as Jesus that he could have been misunderstood and he wanted to avoid that. He was not into the deplorable habit of name dropping. Why should he?

Jesus was not only his brother, Jesus was also his Lord.

On one hand, they may have come from the same earthly family, and for many years they lived together under the same roof; on the other hand, Jude does not want to give any impression of being on an equal footing with Jesus. This man Jude was happy to be a servant of Jesus.

Playing second fiddle

At the same time, he was equally glad to be a servant of others. That was a most demanding role to play on the stage of daily life. It meant he would be second to his brother James in the pecking order, but that did not bother him, he did not lose any sleep over that. James, as we know, was an eminent leader in the early church and his was a household name throughout the land.

It would have been easy for Jude to adopt a spirit of resentment and allow a streak of jealousy to develop between them. That would be natural, it would be understandable; albeit, it would be downright sinful. Jude happily lived under the shadow of his famous brother. That is what being a servant is all about!

What if?

The chances are that Jude was one of the first Jewish Christians to leave Jerusalem during the persecution following the martyrdom of Stephen (*cf.* Acts 8:1, 2).

The early Christian writer Eusebius quotes a story that Jude's grandsons appeared before the Emperor Domitian (AD 81-96), but, 'despising them as of no account, he let them go, and by a decree put a stop to the persecution of the church. But when they were released they ruled the churches because they were witnesses and were also relatives of the Lord.'

I cannot vouch for the historical accuracy of those two stories, they may be nothing more than hearsay. Having said that, one thing I do know, they are a formidable reminder that a godly influence spreads further than we sometimes realise. The same is true when a pebble is thrown into a pond, it is the ripple effect! Believe me, in the muddy and murky waters of today's world, one person can make a difference!

The good news is you do not have to be a Jude or an Einstein to do it! The Bible shows us that God uses ordinary individuals – and very often uses them individually – to do extraordinary things. You could be that person!

3

Count your many blessings!

'... to those who have been called, who are loved by God the Father and kept by Jesus Christ: Mercy, peace and love be yours in abundance.'

verses 1b, 2

Target audience

Jude's succinct 'tract for the times' is addressed to a specific group of people. On the receiving end are those *'who have been called, who are loved by God the Father and kept by Jesus Christ'*.

The trained eye will have detected a triplet in Jude's description of these dear people. And that is fairly common throughout the book, it is a pattern he uses over and over again. (Maybe he was a bit of a preacher in his spare time and he loved a three point outline!)

- In verse 2, for example, Jude greets his readers with a threesome, *'mercy, peace and love'*.

- When, in verses 5-7, he speaks of God's judgment, he gives a trio of illustrations: those who died in the desert after the Exodus, the fallen angels, and the destruction of Sodom and Gomorrah.

- Again, in verse 11, when he speaks of false teachers, he gives a triad of examples: Cain, Balaam, and Korah.

That is only a selection, there are more, and when we come to them in our study, you will recognise them with no difficulty.

A Christian is ...

It seems to me that Jude's opening comments in verse 1 deal with the fundamental question, what is a Christian? I believe, if we get this right, everything else will fall neatly into place. It is crucial, it is foundational.

We have noticed already in Jude's reference to his earthly ties with Jesus that he quickly eliminates that from the salvation scenario. It was not enough for him! For Jude, salvation is more, much more! It is a dynamic spiritual relationship with Jesus Christ, it is a personal intimate partnership with Jesus Christ.

As W H Griffith Thomas once observed, *'Christianity is nothing less and can be nothing more than relationship to Christ.'*

We need to be clear that a Christian is not simply someone who goes to church once a Sunday. A Christian is certainly not just anyone who is privileged to be born of Christian parents, or happens to have been born in a so-called 'Christian' country. By the same token, neither is a Christian someone who lives and operates by the 'golden rule'. Those qualities are all good and highly commendable in themselves, but they do not make you a Christian!

According to Jude, someone who is *'called, loved and kept'* is, in essence, what constitutes a real Christian. These blessings, and countless more, are yours and mine by virtue of our childlike faith in the finished work of Jesus at Calvary.

... called

A Christian is someone who has been *'called'* by God. The Greek word *klētos* means 'an official summons'. A general call to man is issued with the proclamation of the glorious gospel. We can never look at Jesus Christ and conclude that he would not want us (*cf.* John 3:17).

It becomes an effectual call when we positively respond to it. At that moment, we are born and brought into the global family of God. We have been summoned by him because our salvation begins with him doing a deep work of grace in our hearts. He is the one who took the initiative.

C S Lewis is right when he acknowledges that '... *amiable agnostics will talk cheerfully about man's search for God. For me, they might as well talk about the mouse's search for a cat ... God closed in on me.*'

When the divine intruder comes tugging at your heart and mine, it is worth noting that his call always interrupts our usual routine. And in the immediate context of this particular letter, no-one can be called by the holy God and go on living the way they were before. Jude throws down the gauntlet when he implies we cannot follow Jesus Christ and continue uninterrupted in the immoral ways of this world. Jude advocates a clean break with the past! We must put the past behind us. Yesterday (and the day before) is all water under the bridge.

One of Jude's upbeat ideas is that God will continue to call us home until we join him in heaven, and yet it goes even deeper than that.

Christopher Green writes, '*A great truth about Israel in the Old Testament was that they too were called by God to be his people. Jude here writes to Christians who stand in a line of succession which stretches back to God's call of Abraham, through today, to a wonderful future in glory.*'

I think this mind-blowing concept of God's calling is truly beautiful. The Bible teaches us that we have been:

• called to fellowship with the Son in 1 Corinthians 1:9,

• called to inherit a blessing in 1 Peter 3:9,

• called to freedom in Galatians 5:13,

• called to peace in 1 Corinthians 7:15,

• called to holiness in 1 Peter 1:15,

• called to a worthy walk in Ephesians 4:1,

• called to one hope in Ephesians 4:4,

• called to eternal glory in 1 Peter 5:10.

... *loved*

A Christian is someone who is '*loved by God the Father*'. If I were a Scotsman, I would put it like this: such an experience is better felt than telt!

We are loved *by* God and we are loved *in* God!

That is a double guarantee that God's love will not fail us, it will protect us from the outside and it will strengthen us from the inside.

You see, this fantastic truth takes us into the realm of the sublime. It brings us to the threshold of his beneficence and tenderly envelops us in his heart. He loves us dearly. He loves us deeply. We are exceptionally precious to him. It matters to him about you and me. The same love he has shown to Jesus, his one and only Son, he showers upon us. We do not deserve it, but that is love. The good news is, there is nothing we can do to make God love us more than he loves us right now, and there is nothing we can do to make him love us any less.

How you could think so much of us,
And be the God you are,
Is darkness to my intellect,
But sunshine to my heart.

I came across a wonderful saying recently that blessed my heart, let me share it with you: *'God's love for the non-Christian is the broken love of a broken family. God's love for the Christian is the vibrant love of a family in harmony.'*

There is nothing novel or new about this particular aspect of his character. God's unconditional love stretches across both the testaments of Scripture. And yet, it is amazing, there are a number of key passages in the book of Isaiah where the people who are called are also those who are loved. I am thinking of verses like Isaiah 42:6, 43:4, and 44:2.

It is fairly obvious that Isaiah and Jude are on the same wavelength when it comes to a finer appreciation of the love of God. As it was with them, so it is with you and me. It is the love of God which has impacted our hearts and made a world of difference.

... kept

A Christian is someone who is *'kept by Jesus Christ'*. That means our security and safety are his complete concern. It is his responsibility to look after us until the moment when Jesus comes again. The Lord never takes his eye off us for he is constantly watching over us, every minute of every day. He is guarding our footsteps along each mile of the way.

Rejoice! Even though we may fall *on* the rock, we will never fall *off* the rock (*cf.* Psalm 18:2).

In the original language, the word *tēreō* translated *'kept'* is in the perfect tense. It indicates a past completed action that has continuing results. A better rendering of the Greek shows that we are continually kept. In other words, it is an ongoing ministry which he effectively and efficiently implements on our behalf.

We have the grip of God on our lives. The implication is, when we find ourselves in the worst of times, God has not let go of us, and he will not let go of us. In every changing season of life, Christ keeps a firm hold on his people. He has a hand *in* our lives and a hand *on* our lives!

The Puritan commentator, Thomas Manton, says quaintly that *'Jesus Christ is the cabinet in which God's jewels are kept; so that if we would stand, we must get out of ourselves and get into him, in whom alone there is safety.'*

As the people of God, our status is quite unique. We are called by God to be set apart for God so that we might enjoy love with God.

That is something the apostate knows little or nothing about. You see, the Christian is someone who perseveres in the faith, and Christ is the one who keeps us in the faith.

Seeing the big picture

These three terms give us a Christian time-frame. We have been *called*, that refers to God's gracious acts in the past; we are *loved*, that describes his generous attitude to us in the present; and we are being *kept* for a wonderful future with him in endless glory. In a sense, this is a threefold cord, not easily broken.

The God of Abraham praise!

We see a marvellous illustration of these truths in the life of Abraham. In the Bible, the patriarch is generally thought of as the father of those who believe. There is a sense in which Abraham's story is a pattern which is replicated in the life of every child of God.

There came a point in Abraham's life when God *'called'* him to leave his old life of idolatry and moon worshipping and follow him. God gave him a string of wonderful promises which impacted his life and that of his people, and through them, the rest of the world. There were global repercussions to the promises God made to him.

The only reason why God committed himself to Abraham in this way was because he *'loved'* him with a sovereign and special love. Life for him was tough and the road had many twists and turns. Through it all, he proved that his God was one who was able to *'keep'* him in every challenging situation.

Abraham's tale is the thrilling story of all God's people from every generation. It is mine, it is yours, for we are *'called, loved and kept'* by our God!

A God who multiplies!

In verse 2, Jude gives a salutation to his readers. It could be called an embryonic prayer in that it is an impassioned appeal for the Lord to bless them. This comes as a direct consequence of what God has done and is doing for us.

Not only does Jude show us who we are in Christ by saying we are *'called, loved and kept'*, he goes on to remind us of what we have already in Christ. It is his yearning that we may have it in *'abundance'*. He prays that these benefits may be multiplied towards us.

He wants us to grow in our experience of God's favour and blessing, he wants us to move on with God, he wants us to enter into a deepening dynamic relationship with God. That is his dream and aspiration for all the people of God.

Jude knows these tokens of God's goodness will help us to cope in the coming hour of crisis when apostasy seems to be making an inroads into many of our local churches. The graces of our God – mercy, peace, love – defeat the apostate enemy. You see, that is where Jude is earthed to reality and, at the same time, his faith is anchored to the attributes of God.

O S Hawkins makes the valid point that *'the shortest way for sinners to see their need of salvation is to let them see the sanctification of saints!'*

And so, Jude's longing for his readers is expressed like this: *'Mercy, peace and love be yours in abundance'.*

Greetings!

This is a fairly standard shape of greeting. We have come across it many times before, albeit this one is quite unique. If we check back through the greetings which are warmly conveyed in each of the other New Testament letters, we will discover they are generally made up of two or three components. More often than not, they are culled from the familiar trio of grace, mercy, and peace!

Some of them have only two of the elements just mentioned and, where that is the case, these tend to major on grace and peace. That is fine, we do not have a problem there! That was a well-known Jewish form of greeting of the times. The people were *au fait* with it and, therefore, could easily identify with it. It had a contemporary feel to it.

Something extra!

However, this one which Jude is writing adds another dimension to it. He introduces the aspect of love and that is what makes it second-to-none. In fact, that is what gives it a distinctly Christian edge. There is a flavour of Calvary associated with it. Because of this, it seems to add credibility to the idea that Jude was from a Jewish-Christian background.

When we take his beautifully balanced greeting at face value, it tells us much about basic Christian experience. It belongs to the children of God, it is our present possession! We have mercy, peace, and love, and we have them right now!

The question is: how much of them do we have?

Are we running our lives on a half-empty tank?

Like so much in the word of God, there is a lot more to this verse than meets the eye. I believe Jude focuses in verse 2 on an essential truth that many of us have let slip from the moorings of our memory. That is, there are only three basic relationships in life: our relationship with God, our relationship with ourselves, and our relationship with others. We see each of these mirrored in the qualities of *'mercy, peace and love'.*

Merci for mercy!

The first word in Jude's greeting is *'mercy'*. I suppose we can look at it like this: mercy underlines our personal relationship with God. From the extraordinary wealth of his mercy, the Lord freely and fully forgives our sin for he is a God who is 'rich in mercy' (Ephesians 2:4). It is the mercy of God that brings us from the darkness of sin into the wonderful light of knowing Jesus.

The old divines spoke of mercy as the *'darling attribute of deity'*.

Jeremiah reminds us in Lamentations 3:23 that generous tokens of God's mercy are brand spanking new to us every morning as we engage our hearts and minds in communion with him. We feel refreshed and revitalised! It does more for us than having a cold shower! You see, in his mercy, he does not give us what we deserve. The Scots proverb says: 'He is better to the worst of us than the best of us deserve.'

When we experience and enjoy his abundant mercy, we will never be:

• overawed by the power of the enemy,

• overdriven by the pressure of circumstances,

• overstrained by the problems of the task, and

• overweighed by the perils of the way.

Shalom!

The second component in the greeting is *'peace'*. That is an inward experience and it highlights our relationship with ourselves. It is that inner tranquillity in the midst of life's many storms. It is the calm that floods our minds when anxiety is nailed to the cross. It is a deep seated contentment knowing that all is well because God is in control.

You see, the Christian is not someone with whom God is at war, but someone with whom God is at peace. That peace treaty has been signed in Christ's blood shed at Calvary. When we have it, we know it; when it is missing, we know we have lost it!

There is:

• *peace of heart* when there is no condemnation before God,

- *peace of conscience* when there is no controversy with God,
- *peace of mind* when there is no anxiety about life, and
- *peace of action when there is no grit in the machinery.*

The agapē factor

The last ingredient in Jude's triple greeting is *'love'*. As mercy cascades from the Father, peace gushes from the Son, so love streams from the Spirit. This is something which reaches out into the community where we live. It is the natural by-product of a man who has known mercy and who is at peace with himself and God. This should be the hallmark of our churches as we think of the other person's highest good.

Love is the trademark of a genuine and authentic Christianity.

It is the bond that unites believers not only to the Lord but to one another. The word Jude uses for *'love'* is the Greek term *agapē*. It is a brand of love which is unconditional and it even embraces the unlovely and the undeserving. It seems to me that God's love is expressed in his plan to ultimately bring us into his glorious presence. Someone has said it is like the radar system which provides an aircraft with a safe flight path, for it is certain to guide us to our final destination.

Putting it all in perspective

In the immediate context of this chapter, we can see why Jude prayed the way he did. He has a big heart for people. A pastor's heart. A shepherd's heart. He longed to see his people enjoying a well-rounded and close walk with the Lord.

The contrast is patently obvious. These peddlers of error whom Jude is warning of have no real testimony of God's dealings in their lives. For them, life is a soap opera. They operate on a different level, they move on a different plane. They are merchandisers of falsehood as they live a lie themselves.

In comparison to the true Christian, they are mere counterfeits. As common religious criminals, they seek to detract from the glory of the precious, peerless name of Jesus. They are professors of Christianity, but alas, they do not possess the Lord Jesus Christ.

Isn't it great to know, according to Jude, that we have a wonderful Saviour and we have a marvellous salvation. What thrills me is this, it gets better every passing hour! We know it to be gloriously true in our own experience, when we have received the *'mercy, peace and love'* of God through the gospel, that is what God uses to break the heart of the sinner and heal the soul of the saint.

This is what melts our hearts when we first turn to Christ in repentance and faith. This is what sustains us and keeps us going on the journey no matter what life throws at us. If we have his *'mercy, peace and love'* in our lives, we can face the future with confidence, we can cope with the struggles of life.

Going with the flow

We can draw the various strands together and express it like this: when our hearts are filled to the brim, it means:

- *mercy* is the inflow,
- *peace* is the downflow, and
- *love* is the overflow.

4

Apologetics without apology

'Dear friends, although I was very eager to write to you about the salvation we share, I felt I had to write and urge you to contend for the faith that was once for all entrusted to the saints. For certain men whose condemnation was written about long ago have secretly slipped in among you. They are godless men, who change the grace of our God into a licence for immorality and deny Jesus Christ our only Sovereign and Lord.'

verses 3, 4

Believe it or not, Jude is a man in a million. Why is that? Well, he changed his mind!

I was hoping to, but ...

Jude switches topics midstream in his letter. The original burden on his heart, according to verse 3, was to correspond with the believers about their *'common salvation'*. That was something they shared together in the family of God for we are all under the same blood, we are all trusting the same Saviour, and we are all enjoying the same salvation!

In actual fact, we read of his keen enthusiasm for he lets it be known that he was *'very eager'* to pursue that particular line of ministry. I cannot help but wonder how Jude would have developed that spiritually heart-warming theme. We can only surmise and speculate for the time being. When we meet up with him in heaven we can ask him then what was on his mind!

I somehow get the feeling that Jude is not someone who relished controversy. He never courted confrontation. He is not the kind of man who would go out of his way looking for a fight. He had little or no appetite for a spiritual fisticuffs!

Jude preferred to accentuate the positive rather than emphasise the negative.

It would have made life a whole lot easier for him to write a letter rejoicing in the glories of Christ and the privileges which God's people share. That was more his line and that was his preferred option. There are times though when we have to put on the back burner what we would like to do, in order to do what is needed. That is *agapē* love in action!

It was no good shirking responsibility. It may be easier to keep our heads down and hope for the best, but wars are never won like that! He could have ignored the problem and hoped it would go away. But, in the real world, that rarely happens. In the cold light of day, Jude really had no alternative but to follow the prompting of the Holy Spirit. Here was a man led by the Holy Spirit, not his whim.

Jude was a man whose ear was sensitively attuned to the dulcet tones of the voice of God. He is a man whose mind was absorbed and attentive to the unfolding purpose of God.

Because of the closeness of his walk with God, he ascertained there was an inner compulsion weighing heavily on him. It was a kind of internal force which overwhelmed him. The bottom line is that he was a man operating under pressure from the Holy Spirit. The hand of God was resting on him! Jude had what many gospel preachers experience from time to time, an irresistible motivation (*cf.* 1 Corinthians 9:16). All of a sudden Jude put down the harp and picked up the sword.

People matter

You will notice in verse 3 that Jude refers to his unseen audience as *'dear friends'*. I think that is a fascinating phrase and it is one which Paul followed in many of his epistles. The Greek word *agapētos* conveys the idea of a good shepherd caring for his sheep who were in grave danger of straying; it speaks of the concern of a godly elder for those people who were in serious danger of slipping; it refers to the loving compassion of a pastor for the welfare of those who were in acute danger of stumbling.

That is why Jude felt he had to write in the manner he did. It all begins to make sense for here is a man seriously concerned for the truth, controlled by the truth, and motivated by God's honour. Jude feels deeply about those things that God feels deeply about.

Faith matters

What we have in verses 3 and 4 is something of a synopsis where he sets out the theme of his letter in a nutshell. He comes clean, everything is out in the open, he has no hidden agenda, he puts all his cards on the table. People in the pew know precisely where Jude is coming from.

In writing his epistle, Jude succinctly urges them:

*   to *defend* the Faith that some people are *denying*,

*   to *preserve* the Faith that some people are *perverting*, and

*   to *contend* for the Faith that some people are *corrupting*.

There is a vital distinction made in the New Testament between 'faith' and *'the Faith'*. Faith on its own refers to the act of believing. 'The Faith' speaks of the thing which is believed. It is the sum total of revealed truth. It is the final and full revelation of God as we have it in the Bible. To put it simply, the Faith is the word of God.

It is that solid nucleus of truth. There is nothing fluid about it. It is not in a state of flux. As Charles Swindoll points out, 'Unlike modelling clay, it cannot be moulded around each new generation's lifestyles.' Even though God's truth is timeless, it never loses its relevance for it is more up-to-date than this morning's newspaper.

When we turn to the word of God, we have the truth, the whole truth, and nothing but the truth. Such truth not only affects our liturgy, but our lifestyle.

This is something which has been graciously *'entrusted to the saints'*. If you like, we are custodians of the Faith. It was not imparted to human institutions, societies, or organisations, but it was given exclusively to the people of God. We have in our care the oracles of God. And, if the Lord is not going to give us another one, we must guard what we have as highly precious!

The Faith was delivered to the saints; it was not discovered by them!

Jude says the mandate was delivered to us, not once upon a time, but *'once for all'* time. In other words, from God's perspective, there can be no addition to it and there can be no subtraction from it. There is no need for men to supplement or dilute the Christian gospel. In every sense of the phrase, it is a finished work. It is complete!

The same Greek word, *hapax*, is employed in Hebrews 9:26 where a clear reference is made to the absolute finality of the atonement of Christ. We read, 'Then Christ would have had to suffer many times since the creation of the world. But now he has appeared *once for all* (italics mine) at the end of the ages to do away with sin by the sacrifice of himself.'

Thank God, just as there is no more sacrifice needed for sin, so there is no more Scripture needed for the saint.

John Benton writes, 'There is no more new revelation and there is no secret teaching of Jesus we need to know hidden in the sands of an archaeological dig, or in some as yet undiscovered "gospel" locked away in the vaults of a museum.' We have it all!

Defenders of the Faith

As the people of God, our solemn obligation and duty in the third millennium is to wholeheartedly defend the Faith. As we draw closer to the second advent of Jesus, I believe there is an even greater need for us to be combatants and go on the offensive!

- We must stand *for* the truth,
- we must stand *with* the truth, and
- we must stand *by* the truth.

Again, to quote John Benton from his book, *Slandering the Angels*, in the Welwyn Commentary Series: 'We must contend for the Faith whether the gospel is popular or whether it is not. We must do this when society believes in God and when it does not. We must do this when it is intellectually respectable to be a Bible believer and when it is not. We must do it when the established church hierarchy are good men committed to the truth and when they are heretical liberals who sneer at the old gospel. We must do it when Christianity is the dominant faith in a country and when it has to jostle in the religious market-place of a pluralistic society.

'The church must do this whether it is in the midst of a rising civilisation or whether its culture is collapsing all around it. The church must do it in a modern world of science and objectivity and in a post-modern/New Age world dominated by image and subjectivity. The church must do it when it is in the midst of heaven-sent revival or when it is suffering, dwindling, and small.'

Worth fighting for

Like everything in life, there is a proper way to do it! We are to *'contend for the Faith'*. The Greek word favoured by Jude is *epagōnizomai*. It means 'to fight' or 'to struggle' intensely. When we look carefully at the word, we see the root from which it was taken. We get our English word 'agonise' from it!

The picture is one of a wrestling match with a menacing opponent in an ancient gymnasium that is thick and humid with the pungent smell of sweat.

In contending for the truth of the gospel, we must guard against being contentious. The former is frontline fighting with the enemy; the latter, back-stabbing behind the lines within our own troops. The one we are commanded to do (*cf.* verse 3); the other, to avoid (*cf.* Titus 3:9).

We must be ultra-careful not to bring discredit to the cause of Christ. We must take every precaution not to bring disgrace to the character of Christ. We must pull out all the stops lest we bring dishonour to the church of Christ.

Don't drop the baton!

It is a bit like what happens in a relay race where the baton is passed to the front runner from the one coming behind him. Jude reminds us that the baton has been passed to us. It is in our hands today! Our prime responsibility, therefore, is to hand it on to the next generation.

To change the analogy, it is a most worthy cause as we unashamedly nail our colours to the mast. We are soldiers in the Lord's army. We are on the frontline, we are in the trenches. We should be fighting a good fight for the Faith in these days of alarming spiritual decline.

Fact: the church is always one generation short of extinction. If our generation fails to guard the truth and entrust it to our children, then that will be the end!

Know your enemy

When we examine verse 4, Jude is challenging us to know our enemy. These words vividly remind us that the early church had many life-size problems. They had not attained perfection, they were often beset by serious difficulties. Sometimes it was two steps forward and one step back and, from time to time, when they were gallantly standing at the evangelical crease, they found themselves batting on the back foot.

Without naming the *'certain men'* who were poisoning the Christian community, Jude is very direct. An intelligent person could spot them a mile away from Jude's description. Although, it is surprising how indifferent some folk can be.

If the shoe fits

The story is told of the pastor who was greatly upset by a deacon who never applied the sermon to himself but always said, 'Pastor, you sure told them this morning!' As time marched on, a freak rain storm kept all the regular worshippers, except the pastor and deacon, away from the service one Sunday. The pastor preached his heart out knowing the Bible message must hit home this time. After the message, the deacon said, 'You sure would have told them preacher ... if they had been here!'

Jude warns these people without naming them. No doubt, Jude has his reasons for not spelling out who they are. Paul, for example, did not beat about the bush when he exposed Alexander as a man who 'did me a great deal of harm' (2 Timothy 4:14).

Cuckoos in the nest

The dilemma these *'certain men'* caused, as Jude with more than a hint of sarcasm calls them, was designed to wreck spiritual fellowships. They brought in their wake a spirit of dissension and division. The infernal foe was doing more untold damage than the persistent attacks from the enemy outside. There was a cancerous canker eating away at the very heart of the church. But how, you may be asking?

Well, there were those among the Lord's people who had infiltrated their ranks. Like Simon Magus (*cf.* Acts 8:9-25), they were in the church for what they could get out of it. They were intruders. They were active members of Satan's band. They had won over the support of a few with their extrovert personalities and an overdose of charisma. People were conned by the impressive display of these men who were slick and charmingly persuasive in their talk.

They had entered in the disguise of being disciples. They were hiding under the cloak of Christianity. They had joined the church under false pretences. They looked alright on the outside. Nice people! Just as we cannot judge a book by its cover, so we cannot judge a man by his mantle. As Jerry Vines says, 'These people use our vocabulary, but not our dictionary. They use the same words that we use, but they do not mean what we mean by them!'

Under false pretences

Jude says they *'secretly slipped in among'* them. In other words, they did not arrive in the church with a fluorescent placard around their neck saying: 'I am a false teacher'. No! They came in through the back door. There is a stealth and underhandedness to their behaviour. They have insinuated and wormed their way into the congregations because of their adeptness at manoeuvrability. To all intents and purposes, these guys were playing spiritual war-games where subterfuge is an essential tactic.

The word is used to speak of someone who has slipped furtively back into the country from which he has been expelled. It also paints the word picture of an alligator lying on the bank of a river, then slithering into the water so subtly, secretly, and silently, that he is unnoticed. It does not even make a ripple in the water!

In classical Greek literature, the word referred to slipping poison into someone's glass. Charles Swindoll writes, '*As poison dropped furtively into a silver chalice, these men surreptitiously penetrated the church.*'

This was their manner and means of entry. It says a lot about them!

Show-time religion

Jude pulls no punches in verse 4 when he describes them as *'godless'* men. In other words, they are without God. These are individuals who lack reverential awe toward God. On the surface, they may appear to be the kind of people we could do business with. The outward veneer is pleasing to the eye but the heart is quite a different matter. It is as black as coal.

They are 'into' religion and have all the latest gimmicks, they know the choruses, they talk the language, they attend the conferences, they read the magazines, but there is nothing in the heart to win the admiration and praise of an all-seeing God. He sees right through them.

There is an appalling absence of moral restraint in their behaviour for *'they change the grace of our God into a licence for immorality'*. They abuse their liberty making it an excuse for licence.

The devil's purpose behind the false teaching is always somehow to legitimise sin.

These folk have no sense of shame when they commit their evil deeds. They openly flaunt their sin in a spirit of arrogance. By their conduct, they are denying the grace of God. They are carnal from the inside out. And when the camouflage is gone, it shows. Really shows! Their philosophy was simple: don't do as I do, do as I say!

Truth twisters

As synthetic saints, Jude says they *'deny Jesus Christ our only Sovereign and Lord'* and that is always the root of the problem. Jude is deliberately raising the stakes here for their deeds are but a reflection of their doctrine. Both are lacking in reality. Because of what they believed (or did not believe) they had no conscience about their lifestyle. Bad theology often leads to bad morals.

They had no conviction about their pursuit of promiscuity. They reasoned it was a personal matter thereby leaving other people and God out in the cold. What began as an absence of reverence for the Lord and his word resulted in a determined twisting and blatant distortion of the grace of God into an excuse for sin. This culminated and climaxed in an open denial of the person of our Lord Jesus Christ.

- They denied him as *Master* for he is the Lord,
- they denied him as *Mediator* for he is Jesus,
- they denied him as *Messiah* for he is the Christ, and
- they denied him as *Monarch* for he is our only Sovereign.

Such men have looped the loop to such a degree that they could easily hide behind a corkscrew.

When in Rome ...

In Rome, there is a famous building called the Pantheon. One of the best preserved Roman ruins, it was built in 27 BC to serve as the temple to all the gods. In this building there were niches around the walls for all the gods and goddesses of people conquered by the Romans. In this way the Romans appeased their captives.

There was, for example, a niche for the god Jupiter. His followers could come into the Pantheon and worship him. Next to Jupiter was a niche for Juno. In niche after niche after niche, gods were placed around the walls.

When the Romans conquered the Christians, they came up with the bright idea and said, 'We are going to give you a niche for Jesus.' But the Christians were resolute and with a dig-your-heels-in defiance said, 'No! There is only one Lord! There will be no niche for Jesus!' Many believers, young and old, gave their lives for that truth. They were ripped apart by voracious lions and burned at the stake because they insisted that Jesus Christ was the *'only Sovereign and Lord'*.

Forewarned is forearmed

Now we know the enemy! They are Satan's undercover agents. In an age when truth is at a discount, we need to blow their cover and put them out on the pavement to wallow in their sin. They must be exposed and they must be excommunicated from our churches.

This calls for spiritual maturity allied to a biblically informed mind. It requires a loving heart and a firm will. It will take courage and resolve on our part. After all is said and done, the verdict of heaven in verse 4 is that *'their condemnation was written about long ago'*.

Apostasy should not take us by surprise, for God predicted, from the very beginning, that apostates would appear on the scene to do what they do best. They have been around from day one! They go as far back in history as their leader who conned Adam and Eve in the Garden of Eden.

A blast from the past

A quick tour through the Old Testament will reveal many sad instances where apostasy reared its ugly head. In every generation there were always those who voiced opposition to the message proclaimed by God's true servants.

Actually, that was one of the major recurring problems in the days of the Judges. Those days of recycled misery were marked by apostasy and anarchy. Even when the people repented and turned back to the Lord, it was not long before they lapsed and went back to their old ways. As an aside, the book of Judges is not recommended reading if you are feeling under the weather and a little discouraged!

There are many other well-documented cases recorded on the pages of Scripture! For example, Elijah was opposed by the prophets of Baal in 1 Kings 18; Micaiah was opposed by the false prophet Zedekiah in 1 Kings 22; Jeremiah was opposed by the false prophet Hananiah in Jeremiah 28. The Lord himself was vigorously opposed by the religious right in his day.

Reality bites

The fact is the devil is real and there has never been a time when he has not raised up people to stand against the truth of God's word. We need to remember that the devil is no friend to the things of God.

So what is happening today is not a phenomenon unique to the third millennium. It is not new, neither is it unexpected!

It seems to me that it is not only the smooth talker offering health and wealth that we need to worry about, it is also the pin-stripe suited person who dots his intellectual i's and crosses his theological t's; the probability is that both may be working for the same commander. Basically, they are wolves in sheep's clothing!

The words of Edmund Burke serve to underscore the urgency of the situation: *'The only thing necessary for the triumph of evil is for good men to do nothing.'*

5

History repeats itself

'Though you already know all this, I want to remind you that the Lord delivered his people out of Egypt, but later destroyed those who did not believe. And the angels who did not keep their positions of authority but abandoned their own home – these he has kept in darkness, bound with everlasting chains for judgment on the great Day. In a similar way, Sodom and Gomorrah and the surrounding towns gave themselves up to sexual immorality and perversion. They serve as an example of those who suffer the punishment of eternal fire. In the very same way, these dreamers pollute their own bodies, reject authority and slander celestial beings.'

verses 5-8

A little girl complained that she had a sore tummy. 'That's because it's empty! You'll feel much better when you've got something in it,' said her mother. Later that afternoon, during a visit from their minister, he complained of a severe headache. The wee girl perked up and said to him, 'That's because it's empty. You'll feel a lot better when you've got something in it!'

Apart from smiling at the mother's obvious embarrassment when her daughter regurgitated every word she had spoken earlier, there is a truth there for every Christian. As Dr Martyn Lloyd-Jones has said, 'Let us never forget the message of the Bible is addressed primarily to the mind, to the understanding.' You see, cream puff Christianity might taste ever so good, but it will not build you up! That explains Jude's tack in this section.

Memory joggers

Initially, Jude zeroes in on yesterday's men, apostates whose stories have been variously culled from the shimmering mists of antiquity. Even so, these verses are a sobering and salutary lesson for every one of us.

If the truth be told, the lesson we learn from history is that we never learn the lesson from history!

The majority of folk in the early church had forgotten to remember. Sure, their memories were good, the problem was, they were far too short and much too selective for Jude's liking! That is why the apostolic call to remember is vital, especially in our times.

John Benton has observed, *'We live in days in which TV fun-culture encourages us to focus almost exclusively on the here and now. We are the children of an era which sees "progress" as good and the past as obsolete.'* Benton concludes by saying, *'Such an atmosphere stifles inner reflection and breeds social and historical amnesia.'*

I believe his assessment is absolutely right! He hits the nail squarely on the head.

The paralysis of apathy

A man was chatting to his wife at supper when he said to her, 'Honey, did you know the two greatest problems in today's world are ignorance and apathy?' His wife looked at him for a moment and said, 'No, I didn't know and I don't care!'

It seems to me that apathy was public enemy number one in dealing with these rank and file apostates. If we want to immobilise the enemy, we cannot just sit there, twiddling our thumbs, doing sweet nothing! We need to guard against such an attitude lest we relax and get used to the idea. It is perilously simple to opt for the easy life in a foolhardy attempt not to rock the boat.

The chances are, we may prefer to maintain the status quo rather than ruffling a few feathers. It is the mindset which says: 'anything for a quiet life!' Unfortunately, when we have nodded off to sleep in the comfort of our cushioned Christianity, the enemy may have gained a foothold.

Bucking the trend

Therefore, in a serious and valiant attempt to redress the balance, Jude pulls three illustrations from the dusty archives of the Old Testament era. He recognises that his readers are already well aware of the basic Bible stories to which he is going to refer. In one sense, he is tramping down the 'old paths' (*cf.* Jeremiah 6:16) for he is only going to tell them what they already know.

Even though they are well-versed with the biblical narratives, Jude is extremely concerned that they have forgotten the true significance of these incidents. It is not simply the bare facts that they need to grasp, but their meaning. The lessons from each of them need to be assimilated and taken on board. You see, these Old Testament stories are not only fascinating tales of antiquarian interest, each one has a moral attached to it of which we need to take particular note (*cf.* Romans 15:4).

The implication is: we can hear what someone is saying even though we may not be listening!

The three of them are significantly and strategically different. And yet there is a remarkable sameness to each of them. They all have one trait in common. They have one common denominator – they fell! If they do nothing else, they clearly show that rebellion against God does not succeed. To put it simply, we cannot sin and win!

- Israel lost her *victory*,
- the angels lost their *vocation*, and
- Sodom and Gomorrah lost their *virtue*.

By citing these intensely pertinent examples, Jude is hoping that these believers will learn from the past and become overcomers in the future. He does not want them to founder or flounder. He hopes they will not come unstuck when they face a similar situation in their own church. The fact is, they ought to know better.

Israel ... going nowhere

The first illustration is an attempt to square the circle in relation to one nation's encounter with the miraculous. We come face to face with a God who saves, a God who delivers, and a God who liberates. The Lord brought them out of a land of slavery in order to bring them into a place of freedom in a land flowing with milk and honey. It was a step from bondage to blessing.

This was a formative moment for the fledgling nation of Israel, making a rabble of slaves into God's own people. Redeemed from Egypt because they sheltered under the sprinkled blood of the Passover lamb, they now faced the insurmountable hurdle of the Red Sea. And to make matters worse, the enemy was rapidly advancing to the rear and there were high hills on either side. Basically, they were hemmed in.

They were between the devil and the deep Red Sea!

But, you know and I know, God specialises in the impossible. He miraculously opened up the way ahead and, in his providence, he led them through. As they walked through the sandy stretches of desert en route to the promised land, the pilgrims had nothing to lose. In fact, they had everything to gain.

When the border was in sight at Kadesh-Barnea they took cold feet. They were swamped with an air of uncertainty. Doubts nagged and their enthusiasm waned when they heard the biased and blinkered reports from ten of the twelve spies sent out to reconnoitre the land. While they brought back bunches of delicious, mouth-watering grapes, they also spoke of giants stalking the land. The land was lush and fertile, albeit heavily fortified.

When the potentially divisive issue of 'do we go' or 'do we stay' was put to the vote, the majority verdict easily won the day. The people backed down and backed away from responding to the stirring and momentous challenge issued by Joshua and Caleb, the two 'good' spies.

The sons and daughters of Abraham capitulated to their groundless fears and, therefore, were catapulted into an era of watching each other die in the sand dunes!

The result of that epic, fateful, and historic decision was that the Israelites spent the next forty years going round and round in circles in the wilderness (*cf.* Numbers 13:1-14:45).

God has the last word

God's grave displeasure was noticeable in how he handled the situation. Here was a people who had trusted God to bring them out of Egypt but who patently failed to trust the same unchanging God to take them into the land of Canaan. In a sense, they were tying the hands of God behind his back!

Despite the uncountable promises God had given to them, despite the numerous proofs of his stupendous power, when the crunch came and it was make-up-your-mind time, the people, almost to a man, showed an appallingly abysmal lack of faith. Unbelief was their sin and, tragically, it ultimately led to their extermination. Apart from anything else, it kept them out of the place of blessing.

The lesson comes over loud and clear that Jude wants us to grasp.

Privilege brings responsibility.

When God's people sin, he does not view it lightly. He does not smile and say, 'They can't help it, it comes naturally!' He does not take it on the chin and continue doing what he was doing five minutes earlier. Neither does he take it lying down. Because of who he is, and in order to remain true to himself and his character, he has no option but to do something about it!

Against the tide

The gauntlet is thrown down to the believers in the early church not to go with the flow of error but to bravely swim against the tide and repel the foes of darkest apostasy. If they buried their head in the sand by failing to grasp the nettle and deal with the spiralling situation, it would bring its own self-inflicted consequences. That is why faith is so crucial.

In the twenty-first century, we live in a culture which is saturated with the twin towered influences of atheism and agnosticism. The mass media, including cyberspace, is dominated by these ideas. The prevalent lifestyle of our Western world is geared towards worshipping the god of materialism. We are hedonistic in the extreme. In such a secular, sybaritic environment, our faith is constantly being challenged.

We often hear so-called enlightened people saying: *'You can't really believe that old gospel from that old Bible! That's old hat!'*

Even though a hostile, less-than-sympathetic press may caricature us as intellectual lightweights and fuddy-duddy obscurantists, it is possible for us to maintain a sense of equilibrium in our relationship with the Lord Jesus Christ and, with the same grit and determination, to follow him intelligently every day. That never-say-die attitude shows we have learned the lesson from the Israelites that Jude speaks of in verse 5. As they say, once bitten, twice shy!

Angels ... going down

The second of Jude's memory jogging illustrations in verse 6 takes us even further back in the annals of time. In fact, we move out of the terrestrial realm into the celestial where we are invited to ponder the judgment of fallen angels. We move into the invisible spiritual world of angelic beings.

It is not unreasonable to assume that these angels despised their rank and wilfully rejected the divine claim on their created powers. Of their own volition, these exalted beings abandoned their lofty heights of power and dignity. They chose to opt out of the purpose of God for them.

If the children of Israel went walk-about, then the angels walked out!

Some commentators feel this is a reference to the original fall of the angels when they followed Satan in open rebellion against the Most High God. We have tantalising glimpses of their attempted and spectacularly botched *coup d'état* in Isaiah 14:12-15 and Ezekiel 28:11-19.

It seems more likely, however, bearing in mind the context of what Jude is saying, that the angels in question were not entirely satisfied with the role God had allocated to them and they infringed the boundaries by intermarriage with human beings.

What I understand from these verses is that fallen angels came to earth during the days of Noah and had sexual relations with women, thus producing a race of giants that the Bible refers to as Nephilim. This was one reason God destroyed the world using the flood during Noah's day. The incredible account of this event is recorded for posterity in Genesis 6:1-4.

The bottom line is they deserted the heavenly realm in a token gesture of rebellion and they paid dearly for it. It is worth noting Jude's play on words here as he illuminates the story with a grim pun. These angels, itching for lust, could not *'keep'* to their place. But God will not be rebelled against, and he has *'kept'* those same angels to face judgment at some point in the future.

In other words, if the angels cannot do what they are supposed to do, God can!

Behind bars

Their doom is sealed. They do not get away with it, they do not get off scot-free! They cut themselves off from everything that might have been theirs. They have remained for thousands of years in the nether gloom *'bound with chains'* awaiting their ultimate sentencing on the day of judgment. In the words of William Gurnell, 'None sink so far into hell as those who come nearest to heaven because they fall from the greatest height.'

The passing of time has not lightened or lessened their eventual fate. If anything, it underlines the seriousness of their revolt. Jude is vividly depicting the misery of their conditions. Free spirits and celestial powers, as once they were, are now shackled and impotent. Shining ones, once enjoying the marvellous light of God's glorious presence, are now plunged in profound darkness.

These pits of terrible, deep, dense black *'darkness'* in the unseen world are compared to underground caverns; it is a kind of subterranean region where God has them under lock and key until the scheduled day of accountability (*cf*. 2 Peter 2:4). God's judgment, then, is inescapable, even though it may be delayed.

For these highly privileged angels, in the words of John Bunyan, they found *'at the gates of heaven, there was a way to hell!'*

You see, both men and angels are subject to the word of God. God's law stands and we are under its authority. It stands above the world, above time, and above all earthly cultures. Because God's truth is eternal and does not change, that is why Jude calls us to wake up and get our act together. If we (like the angels) allow pride and lust to rule our lives, we are in danger of losing our victory and our vocation!

Sodom and Gomorrah ... gone!

The third illustration in verse 7 deals with the townsfolk of Sodom and Gomorrah. These folk lived in an ideal environment that was stunningly beautiful and fabulously prosperous. It has been compared to the idyllic setting of the 'garden of the Lord' (*cf.* Genesis 13:10). That is what makes the panoramic sweep of God's judgment upon these unsuspecting individuals all the more breathtaking and mind blowing.

If the people of Jude's day failed to appreciate the significance of the previous couple of incidents, this one should make the hair stand on the back of their neck. It should send the shivers down their spine.

Where reputation counts for nothing

The twin towns of Sodom and Gomorrah, together with their satellite settlements of Admah and Zeboiim, are infamous for one particularly heinous sin, the odious sin of homosexuality. God was repelled by their despicable behaviour and animal-like relationships. It smelt like a foul pungent aroma in his nostrils. It was vulgar. It was vile.

From God's perspective, the gay life was not the good life.

Their shockingly horrible acts underlined the total depravity of man. He had sunk to the depths of base carnality. He had plummeted to the gutter of sordid seamy relationships. When Jude's insightful comments are read alongside the factual account recorded in Genesis 19 it appears that we are talking about an attempted homosexual gang rape. Surely we can begin to appreciate what Paul meant when he said in Romans 1:28 that 'God gave them over to a depraved mind, to do what ought not to be done.'

You see, when people go too far in sin, God gives them over to their sin! Does God sit idly by while men sin with men and replace virtue with vice? He certainly does not!

Sixty minutes later ...

God in his holiness was determined to avenge. And he did! We read in Genesis 19:24 that 'the Lord rained down burning sulphur on Sodom and Gomorrah.' Result: the cities of the entire plain fell. They became a smouldering heap of rubble. Now you see them, now you don't!

Fire and brimstone rained upon these red light communities with the sole purpose of bringing about their liquidation from the face of the planet. Inside one hour, God wiped these dens of homosexuality off the earth.

Archaeologist, Dr Melvyn Grove Kyle, led an expedition to a site at the southern end of the Dead Sea where the ancient name Sodom is preserved in a place called Jabal Usdum, or Mount Sodom. He tells how he found ruins of an old city of Canaan definitely identified as Zoar on an elevation toward the east. Kyle concludes that the ruins of Sodom now lie beneath the waters near the shore of the Dead Sea.

As silt has been deposited in the north by the Jordan River, the water has gradually encroached upon the southern bank, covering the site where stood the ancient cities of Sodom, Gomorrah, Admah, and Zeboiim. This entire area is a burnt-out region of oil and bitumen.

Genesis 11:3 and 14:10 are said to have supplied the clue to the presence of oil which led to the discovery of the great Near Eastern oil fields. Old descriptions of the Dead Sea refer to the presence of floating masses of bitumen on its surface.

A great rupture in the earth's strata, dating from Zoar's day, and the presence of vast quantities of sulphur and salt scattered over the region as though by a tremendous cataclysm have led geologists to conclude that there was once a terrific explosion in a subterranean pool of oil near the southern shore of the Dead Sea.

That intervention of God, when he used an horrific fireball in an act of righteous judgment, was only a prelude to their ultimate doom in eternity. It was only the curtain raiser to their guaranteed fate at the end of time. These sexually degenerate reprobates virtually signed their own death warrant. They consigned themselves to the condemned cell. The lesson is clear: if we play with fire, we will get badly burned.

Wake up!

Jude, in bringing these three illustrations to prominence, is hoping those who tune in to his message will be shocked and shaken to their senses. If we ignore the words of Jude, there is no hope for the church. Whether we realise it or not, we are only one generation away from shutting up shop. This should make every true believer a dedicated soul winner and an ardent and loyal defender of the Faith. You see, false teachers are successful because Christian people are ignorant. The baseline is that God has done it before and he may yet do it again.

Billy Graham is credited with the statement: *'If God doesn't punish America, he will have to apologise to Sodom and Gomorrah!'*

The cartoon said it all! A sophisticated college student was speaking to a missionary unmistakably identified by his proverbial pith helmet and shorts. Bewildered, the student asked, 'But what do you do when you can't take the superstition and violence and immorality any longer?' 'Simple,' came the reply, 'we get on a plane and go back to the mission field!'

Ouch! Every day the media shouts the message that we would rather not hear. The lights go out in a great city and an orgy of lawlessness results. Derek Stringer believes that 'ours is a cut-flower civilisation'. While a sign of life remains, we have cut ourselves off from our biblical roots, and the petals are beginning to droop and fall.

It seems to me that the fabric of our society is unravelling before our eyes. The foundations are crumbling. Standards are falling. We are in dire straits. We are overwhelmed by a tidal wave of immorality and amorality. The message of Jude has never been more relevant than it is right now! We need to listen to his alarm call and heed his solemn warning: Remember Sodom!

Losers, every time

The three cameos we have looked at in Jude provide us with a highlighted prototype of God's attitude. We can put it like this:

- Israel *disbelieved* and lost her *power*,
- the angels *disobeyed* and lost their *position*,
- Sodom and Gomorrah were *defiled* and lost their *purity*.

At the end of the day, sin is sin is sin. On the balance sheet of life, it is an incalculable loss and an eternal liability.

Some things never change

We have the punchline in verse 8 when Jude says history repeats itself. This is a rerun of things that have happened before. As it was, so it is! That is precisely what was happening in Jude's day. And we have gone full circle in our present generation. We are back to the days Jude graphically portrayed in the preceding verses as he begins his unequivocal statement by declaring *'in the very same way'*.

When the curtain is drawn aside we catch a glimpse of the dominant features in their character. But we also notice the domineering factors in their conduct. They are the best of a bad bunch. What are they guilty of?

Dream on ...

Jude in a no-punches-pulled statement calls these folk, *'dreamers'*. The word Jude uses, *enupniazō*, means 'a confused state of the soul or an abnormal imagination, producing dreams in which the ego is controlled and held captive by ungodly, sensual confusion'.

In other words, they live in a world of make believe. They often embark on fanciful flights of imagination taking them into the fluffy clouds of sensual fantasy. Their homespun philosophy is pie-in-the-sky as they blatantly defy all logic and reason. They show a wilful disregard for recognised moral and ethical standards. They seem happy enough to operate in uncharted waters.

Their thought life is poisoned as they subject themselves to demonic influence. Because their mind has become a cesspool of iniquity they have no conscience about their despicable activities. Their inner warning voice is seared because they are wallowing in a filthy sewer. Theirs is the religion of the gutter. Sin is a way of life to them, and the more obscene the better. Virtue has long since gone, it has flown through an open window. They are held firmly in the grip of vice.

As they attempt to satisfy the appetite of the flesh they indulge in the works of the flesh.

The logo emblazoned on the lapel of their lives is Eros.

Irrespective of how unnatural the physical relationship may be they plunge deeper and deeper into the bottomless pit of sin. Their bodies and minds have become pawns in the hand of Satan. They are sold out to the devil. They engage in impassioned displays of lewdness and the more crude the better. Their outlook is one of free love for all.

Free from the law

Jude makes it clear in the next phrase that they *'reject authority'*. In that sense, they are lawless and, generally speaking, such individuals tend to be a law unto themselves anyway. When operating in reject mode, they have no respect whatsoever for either political or ecclesiastical authority.

Their policy is simple: rules are made to be broken.

Just because a law was tabled in the word of God, or a statute written into a nation's constitution, that did not matter one iota.

They were hell-bent in their pursuit of carnal recklessness. They imbibed a spirit of revolt and anarchy as they embraced warmly the concept of total freedom with no restrictions attached. It was, in reality, a concession to licence. Because of their attitude and actions, they are antichrist in their heart. They are intractable as they fly in the face of law and authority.

Without doubt, the setting aside of the authority of Scripture is incorporated in the phrase we are thinking about. Apostates cast to the ground the word of God and trample it under foot. Hand in hand with the spurning of God's precepts is the call for a new social order. It is a civil rights charter.

Thus the phrase supplies a key to the otherwise inexplicable fact that many apostate religious leaders are often associated with subversive organisations which seek to undermine and orchestrate attempts to overthrow governments.

They are happy to pronounce their pastoral blessing on freedom fighters and those who engage in long struggles for independence based on their warped liberation theology.

The reason why these impostors reject authority is because they have no wish to permit Jesus Christ to govern in their lives. They do not want to be boxed in by any biblical parameters. They do not want a God who rules over them.

Big mouths

Theirs is a life of derisive contempt as they degrade dignitaries. Every time they open their mouth they *'slander celestial beings'* and speak evil against the Most High God. They blaspheme by lip as they engage in cynicism, ridicule, and short-sighted verbal abuse. According to Derek Stringer, 'the only time that they seriously fall to their knees is when they are looking for their lost contact lenses.'

In a word, they have no respect for God's appointed leaders nor do they esteem God's anointed messengers.

They have swallowed hook, line, and sinker, the bait that Satan has tempted them with. They have fallen headlong into the trap he has set and now they are his willing henchmen. That spirit of apostasy found in Jude's day is abroad in these last days. Looking around us, I sometimes wonder if the complete fulfilment of Jude's prophecy is near.

* In *body*, these apostates are immoral,
* in *soul*, they are insubordinate, and
* in *spirit*, they are irreverent.

I think it is absolutely clear from Jude's sharp cutting edge teaching in verses 5 to 8 that the new morality we hear so much about today is nothing more than the old immorality wrapped in a different package.

Dalmatian theology

Men do not reject the Bible because it contradicts itself but because it contradicts them! An historical review of biblical scholarship during the past century will reveal that the first to undermine the great doctrines of grace and glory have been those within the church. Needless to say, the damage they have caused has been enormous. Much of the rejection of Christianity today is built on the rejection of yesterday. The theology on offer is a 'Dalmatian' theology, one holding that the Bible is inspired only in spots!

Francis Schaeffer was right when he said that 'historic Christianity and either the old or the new liberal theology are two separate religions with nothing in common except certain terms which they use with totally different meanings.'

When it comes to an apostate, the question is: *'can a leopard change its spots?'*

6

Naming and shaming

*'But even the archangel Michael, when he was disputing with the
devil about the body of Moses, did not dare to bring a slanderous
accusation against him, but said, "The Lord rebuke you!" Yet these
men speak abusively against whatever they do not understand; and
what things they do understand by instinct, like unreasoning animals
– these are the very things that destroy them. Woe to them! They
have taken the way of Cain; they have rushed for profit into
Balaam's error; they have been destroyed in Korah's rebellion.'*

verses 9-11

How to treat the devil!

The main beam in verse 9 is shining on the trio of Moses, Michael, and the
devil. By any stretch of the imagination, that is a highly unusual combination!
It seems a strange verse for here we have a fact not disclosed anywhere else
in Scripture. It deals with the skilful handling of Satan by Michael the
archangel.

According to the early Christian writer Origen, Jude is here referring to
a fascinating story that is told in a highly readable volume called *The
Assumption of Moses.* The manuscript of this piece of apocryphal Jewish
literature still exists. Cerani discovered a large fragment of a Latin version
in the Ambrosian library in Milan. The Latin version was translated from a
Greek text, and the original was probably in Hebrew or Aramaic.
Unfortunately, the part of the book that Jude quotes from is missing

Angelic pecking order

The name *'Michael'* means 'one who is like God'. In other words, the angel was a reflector of the glory and beauty of the Lord. He got like the company he kept!

Michael was the manager of the heavenly host and held a position of supreme authority. Having scaled to the top rung of the ladder in terms of angelic rank, Michael has overall responsibility for the day to day administration of the angelic band. He oversees all appointments within the heavenly realm and supervises all arrangements regarding specialised roles (*cf.* Revelation 8). In this capacity, he is still fully responsible to the throne of God.

A set-to with the devil

Did you notice what Michael is doing? He is *'disputing with the devil'* in relation to the whereabouts of the body of Moses. The terms used in this passage are forensic, they are the language of the courtroom.

The tradition was that Michael came down from heaven to get Moses' body in order to escort it back to heaven. When he arrived, the devil said, 'You can't take this body to heaven because this man was a murderer!' The devil seems to have accused Moses of being unworthy of heaven by resurrecting the memory of a past wrong.

Wherever Michael is mentioned in the Bible it is, nine times out of ten, in relation to the nation of Israel and the Jewish people. He emerges on the canvas of Scripture as their guardian angel and that is especially appropriate in the dark days of the Tribulation (*cf.* Daniel 10:13, 12:1).

On this occasion, however, Michael is embroiled in a slightly different role, a role that is quite unusual for him. The devil is up to no good! He is loitering with intent as he makes a few dubious enquiries about the locale of the *'body of Moses'*. Guess what? Michael is on the receiving end!

The devil is a rather inquisitive old so-and-so.

I need hardly remind you that his motives are always ulterior. So far as I am aware, there is only one reference in Scripture to the body of Moses and that leads us to believe that God is the only one who knows where his servant is buried.

When Moses reached the grand old age of 120 years, the narrative informs us: 'And Moses the servant of the Lord died there in Moab, as the Lord had said. He buried him in Moab, in the valley opposite Beth Peor, but to this day no-one knows where his grave is' (Deuteronomy 34:5, 6).

The biblical record clearly implies the precise location of Moses' tomb is unknown to man and angel. This time, Satan is out in the dark. God has hoodwinked him.

This was a no-go and a no-*know* area for the wily devil.

It is well within the bounds of possibility to suggest that if the actual burial site had been revealed to man it would have become the object of much veneration. There is no doubt that it would have rapidly turned into some kind of shrine to be visited by the devotees of many religions. I reckon it would have become another popular venue on the merry-go-round itinerary of money spinning pilgrimages!

Silence is golden

Michael's reaction and response says it all. He knew when to keep his mouth shut. He did not lower himself in any way nor did he get involved in a slanging match with the enemy. Even though the devil was in the wrong, Michael graciously refrained from addressing personal rebuke to him. He could have attempted to vindicate himself or perhaps he could have questioned the authority and motives of Satan, but he did not. He clicked his heels and bluntly said, *'the Lord rebuke you'*.

You see, Michael was quite content to leave the eventual outcome with the Lord. Judgment is a divine prerogative. That is his domain. The Lord can settle every issue. And, given time, he will.

Think twice before jumping in with both feet

I think it is vitally important for us to realise that it is a precarious thing for God's people to confront Satan directly and to argue with him. The fact is, the adversary is much stronger than we are. If an archangel is careful about the way he deals with the devil, how much more cautious ought we to be!

William Barclay writing in the *Daily Study Bible* expresses the opinion that Jude means, 'If the greatest of the good angels refused to speak evil of the greatest of the evil angels, even in circumstances like that, surely no human being may speak evil of any angel.'

It is gloriously true that we share in the victory and triumph of Jesus at Calvary; it is equally true that we must not be presumptuous.

The man is a fool who thinks he can play around with the devil and treat him with kid gloves.

Satan is a dangerous enemy and, when we resist him, we must be sober and vigilant at all times (*cf.* 1 Peter 5:8, 9).

Men with four legs

I think you will agree with me when I say that Jude's description of these impostors in verse 10 is both weird and gripping. It is quite sensational for ordinary grown men to be labelled and libelled the way they are.

They are an affront to society for they are acting like beasts. The harsh reality is, sometimes they are a lot worse than that! And when that happens, it is the animals that deserve an apology!

In their sexual immorality, they are gallivanting all over the place like horses or dogs on heat unable to control their desire.

Every well-rehearsed pronouncement they make from their ivory towers is pernicious. They cannot say anything good about God or man so they indulge in a concerted propaganda campaign of evil. Jude says their defamatory language is *'abusive'* as they blaspheme and reproach.

Ignorance is not bliss

The amazing thing is that they are lecturing and pontificating on what Jude says are things *'they do not understand'*. In other words, they are where they are because they are self-elected and self-appointed. They have a high opinion of themselves! These guys are acting in such a manner because they reckon they know it all.

They present themselves in public and in private as the fount of all knowledge. Yet, in the cold light of every new day, they are intellectual eggheads. They are dunces. They have not got a clue about anything as they rant and rave to anyone who is foolish enough to listen. It is the blind leading the blind on a ramble through the maze of ill-conceived scatter-brained thoughts of these men.

Even though they did not know what they were talking about, they knew exactly what they were doing. That came naturally. The herd instinct rose to the surface. And, tragically, that is what they followed. They are men with four legs.

Burnout!

Bear in mind, these are synthetic saints Jude is talking about here. These are apostates that Jude is collaring. Real people! Their sinful acts, their vulgar vices, their gross immorality, their total disregard for any of the laws of nature, made them worse than the heathen pagans all around them.

With their crass behaviour, they had sunk to the lowest of the low. In all honesty, they could not sink much further. Their fate is inevitable and well-catalogued. Jude says *'these are the very things that destroy them'*. They are programmed for certain doom. They are pressing their personal self-destruct button. Lust is a lethal weapon, and when indulged, it is a killer!

Alright, if we play with fire, we will get badly burned. That is what happened to them! Their lust burned within them and they destroyed themselves. They burned themselves out. Sin when left to run its course will take a man to the lake of fire.

It seems to me from Jude's earlier comments that sin will stain a man, spoil a man and, ultimately, slay a man.

These folk are firmly held in the tentacles of the enemy and they cannot break free from his clutches. Therein lies the peril of men turning their back on God. Is it any wonder Jude says what he does?

Staying clean in a dirty world

It is abundantly clear that the world of the apostate is a murky one. The atmosphere is eerie. That is why as real believers we must consciously guard the purity of our church fellowships and keep ourselves unspotted from the sinful influences of the world. We cannot afford to become contaminated or polluted with those who pander to the flesh in the name of religion. They talked about what they do not know; as believers, we must talk about what we do know!

Following them inevitably leads to destruction because they are going after sin which is like a Semtex high explosive that cannot be defused. It will blow them up! Only Christ and his cross can defuse it. That is the ignorance of the false teachers!

A spade is a spade!

There is one thing I really admire about our friend Jude, he does not beat about the bush nor does he go around the world for a short-cut.

A patient visited the surgery of his doctor. *'Tell me without a long scientific name what is wrong with me, doctor, I can take it,'* he said. The doctor gave him that once-over look and replied, *'Your problem is that you are just plain lazy.'* The patient responded, *'Thanks, doctor, now will you give me the long scientific name so I can tell the family!'*

Jude tells it as it is without embellishment. At this juncture, Jude moves on a stage where he wants to point out just how dangerous these men are and how virulent is their error.

They encapsulate all the worst characteristics of false teachers. We need to be aware that it is not a standard case of one size fits all. There are different types of false teachers. There is nothing stereotyped about them. They have not been mass produced on an assembly line!

Some of them are like number one, that was Cain; some of them are like number two, that was Balaam; some of them are like number three, that was Korah; others come along and they are a combination of two or more of them.

This erstwhile trio is the antithesis of the Lord Jesus Christ. They are diametrically opposed to him, for example:

- instead of the *way* of Christ, there is the *way* of Cain,
- instead of the *truth* of Christ, there is the *error* of Balaam, and
- instead of the *life* of Christ, there is the *death* of Korah.

We fall into a great trap if we think all false teachers are tarred with the same brush. Jude does not claim immunity from prosecution as he launches feet first into a most enlightening presentation of some golden oldies who were apostate in their thinking. We delve back into the dim and distant past as Jude focuses on a trio of characters well known for their movements and mistakes. They are thumbnail sketches, collated from the dusty archives of antiquity, of a handful of men who fell by the wayside. Oliver Wendall Holmes Jr. writes, 'When I want to understand what is happening today or try to decide what will happen tomorrow, I always look back.'

Jude is not afraid to name names when he calls them for what they are! It is what the spin doctors call in today's politically correct climate, the well-honed art of naming and shaming!

- Cain was an arable farmer,
- Balaam was a prophet, and
- Korah was a prince.

That implies apostasy is not confined or restricted to any particular class of people. Every strata of society is embraced here. It touches the common man in the street, it touches the cleric in his religious fiefdom, and it touches the upper crust who stalk the corridors of power.

In the words of S. Maxwell Coder, *'There are apostates in the pulpit, in the palace, and in the poorhouse!'*

The men Jude is talking about have not only secured access into the local church, they have gained ascendancy. They effectively hijacked the local leadership. Theirs was not an abortive coup. They were not the backroom boys nor were they members of the back seat brigade. They were functioning as teachers who were actively pursuing a course that would brainwash and indoctrinate their pupils.

Running scared

It is fairly obvious what God thinks about the emerging scenario. The attitude of heaven is crystal clear. Jude says in verse 11, *'woe to them!'* That is strong language indeed. Those are terse and powerful words. Yes, these men incur the wrath of God upon their souls.

Jude does not play around with words in an attempt to soft soap them. He is not being vindictive or splenetic. He is only telling the truth, the whole truth, and nothing but the truth. God is against them! The Greek word *ouai* translated '*woe*' speaks of a culmination of calamity, pathos, hopelessness, and sorrow. It is a crisp emphatic denunciation.

Their destiny is ominous. The future for these religious cranks is full of foreboding. And to make matters worse, there is no prospect of recovery in the long term. They have seriously overstepped the mark and they have gone well beyond the point of no return. Once this act of spiritual treachery takes place and the sentence is announced, it is irrevocable, it is final. No plea of mitigating circumstances will be heard. They have brought it on themselves and they have no-one else to blame.

Not the shortest straw

To skim across the surface of the verse it would appear that Jude is picking a few individuals out of the hat at random. That is not the case for they were selected by the Holy Spirit because of their eminent suitability.

Individually, they speak of one aspect of what it means to fall away from the truth; when taken together, as a threesome, they present a more complete and fuller picture.

There is nothing static in the biblical text. There is no hint of a halt or a turning back. No U-turn is anticipated. It is recklessly hurtling down the slippery slope to hell. It is a vicious circle and it should serve as a terse warning to those operating on the fringes of the fellowship.

Apostates, first of all, enter upon a wrong path, then they run rapidly down that road, and finally, they perish at the end of it. They are like a runaway car careering dangerously down a steep gradient.

- They *tampered* with the truth, then
- they *twisted* the truth, then
- they *turned away* from the truth.

The sad reality is, this is the life and death of a synthetic saint!

- They pervert the worship of Christ in *mode*, that was Cain;

- they pervert the worship of Christ in *motive*, that was Balaam;
- they pervert the worship of Christ in *manner*, that was Korah.

Rebellion against the way to God

Jude points his index finger at these apostates and declares they have *'taken the way of Cain'*. The story is told in Genesis 4:1-7 and it provides us with an account of one of the first worship services in human history. Cain thinks his way is better. He feels it is more palatable and, consequently, he reckons it is a more acceptable way to do business with God.

Basically, Cain was guilty of rationalism.

We can imagine his reaction when God responded in the manner in which he did. Cain was absolutely humiliated! He felt aggrieved and dejected when God rejected his offering and accepted his brother Abel's instead.

Actually, the major difference between the two offerings was the blood. Cain set aside the blood of sacrifice and thought he could still gain access into the presence of the Lord. He believed God would be well pleased and satisfied with the top quality agricultural produce of his hands. The fact is, Cain wanted to do his own thing and he wanted to go his own way. He sought to get the upper hand and play a game of one-upmanship in his attitude towards the God of heaven.

We know the sequel to the story when in a fit of pique and with a highly cynical attitude Cain eliminated his younger brother. With Abel's death, we have the first recorded incident in Scripture of fratricide.

The way of Cain is with us today! It was General William Booth – founder of the Salvation Army – who said that the chief danger facing the modern church was to proclaim *'a religion without Christ, a salvation without regeneration, and a heaven without hell.'*

Rebellion against the walk with God

Other fervent flimflammers have jumped on the fast-moving bandwagon and *'rushed for profit into Balaam's error'*. That is how Jude describes his voracious greed in verse 11. The hapless story of Balaam is chronicled in Numbers 22-24. He was a prophet who was in it for profit!

To me, one of the tragedies of his story is that he was one of the best-informed Gentiles about God's plan for Israel, yet his crazy decision meant that he is last heard of in a printout recording the names of those who perished in battle (*cf.* Joshua 13:22).

Balaam used his spiritual insight to obtain material gain. He lined his own pockets at the expense of other people. He compromised his status and he devalued the ministry God had given to him. Derek Stringer believes that 'the sin of Balaam was to say the right things when pressed but to mix with the wrong people. He could be orthodox in his prophecies but he was the great compromiser in his associations. Balaam thought that sound theology compensated for everything.'

Balaam's error was not just in doing what he did, but in thinking that he could get away with it. In modern speak, it means these men put a price on their ministry.

Money is the baseline. If the price is right, they would do anything and they would go anywhere. They were preaching for what they could get out of it, a big fat cheque at the end of a church service. So far as they were concerned, it had nothing to do with faith, but it had a lot to do with a fee. For these men, money talks!

These folk knowingly sacrificed eternal riches for temporal benefits. They exercised a compelling desire to acquire some part of the world even at the expense of losing their own soul. They were in the dock for milking believers dry for the sake of hard cash and dollar currency. They stifled their own convictions for short-lived gain.

Rebellion against the worship of God

Apostates are also likened to the much vaunted rebellion of Korah which is amply recorded in Numbers 16. He was into egalitarianism among God's people in a big way! You will remember he is the fella who, in cahoots with others, planned an insurrection against the leaders of Israel. Basically, it was anarchy! Along with some of his misguided peers, he hatched a plot to overthrow the Lord's servants. They wanted to ditch Moses (God's prophet) and Aaron (God's priest).

Their ulterior motive was fired and fuelled by jealousy. The wisecrack of a comedian was, 'My wife's jealousy is getting ridiculous. The other day she looked at my calendar and wanted to know who May was.'

The fact is, jealousy is no joke. It is the raw material of murder. Jealousy is the easiest thing to see in somebody else but the hardest to detect in yourself.

He felt they were doing the nation a big favour. In reality, they were standing against the mind and purpose of God and they paid a high price for their crass stupidity. He made a huge impact but it did not last for long! You see, when we throw mud at another person, we lose ground!

They contravened God's law and, because of that, they carried the can. God had the last laugh! The ground opened in a moment and, to a man, they all perished. The earth swallowed them up. God vindicated his servants. He always does. It was A B Simpson who said, 'I would rather play with forked lightning or take in my hands live wires than speak a reckless word against any servant of Christ.'

Think about it: what started out as freethinking sin with Cain and turned into an undermining weakness with Balaam now becomes a full-scale revolt with Korah.

We can summarise it like this:

- Cain *ignored* the word of God,
- Balaam *opposed* the word of God, and
- Korah *rebelled* against the word of God.

United we stand

The alarming tendency today in evangelical circles is to fragment and break up into all shapes and sizes of groups. It seems to me that little meetings filled with discontented church members soon become an ideal breeding ground for party political activists to wave their distinctive banner. Splits in church fellowships are happening virtually every week around the country as men gather a few 'yes' men around them and begin to build their own empire.

I can tell you, God is not amused, he is not impressed. Those of us who love the Lord must endeavour to keep the unity of the Spirit in such a manner that befits the gospel of Christ (*cf.* Ephesians 4:3). It seems to me that these three illustrations inspirationally culled from a past generation are most relevant to the church in the third millennium.

They show us that even though there may be new faces, their errors and their ways are as old as the hills.

Sound familiar! So it should for Solomon in his wisdom coined the phrase: 'there is nothing new under the sun!'

7

Spitting image

'These men are blemishes at your love feasts, eating with you without the slightest qualm – shepherds who feed only themselves. They are clouds without rain, blown along by the wind; autumn trees, without fruit and uprooted – twice dead. They are wild waves of the sea, foaming up their shame; wandering stars, for whom blackest darkness has been reserved for ever.'

verses 12, 13

A suburban church minister explained to the famous American evangelist, D L Moody, that he would love to have him preach to the congregation, but he considered it unwise as he had a difficult people! He feared that many of them would get up and walk out halfway through the sermon. Moody said that he was willing to run the risk.

Introducing his message, Mr Moody said, *'The first half of my sermon will be for all the sinners here. The second half will be for all the saints. Feel free to leave when you feel that I have spoken to you.'* Everybody stayed for the end of the message!

All that Jude states in the middle section of his epistle is about the sinner but to the saint! The punters tell us that one picture is worth a thousand words! That explains why Jude deploys a quintet of figures-of-speech in this duo of verses in a pivotal attempt to show these infiltrators in their true colours.

Thomas Fuller reckoned that *'similes are the windows which give the best lights.'*

Jude unmasks them by bringing before us five nightmare pictures in a montage of images which we shall find hard to forget. In his skilful use of illustration, Jude has already covered the whole of creation ranging from angels, to men, to animals. Nature is the missing link.

Here, in the space of a couple of verses, he makes amends! If you like, these are windows on the world of nature.

• He gives us a glimpse of the earth which shows their lack of *peace*,
• he looks at the air which reveals their lack of *productivity*,
• he refers to the trees which highlights their lack of *proof*,
• he speaks about the sea which emphasises their lack of *purity*, and
• he reflects on the starry heavens which focuses on their lack of *purpose*.

Holed below the water line

Jude says, first and foremost, these false teachers are *'blemishes at your love feasts'*. Another translation of this phrase depicts them as hidden rocks or sunken reefs. In all fairness, that is more in keeping with the Greek word *spilas* which, interestingly enough, is used only here in the New Testament.

An apostate is, therefore, like the tip of an iceberg!

Very little of their spurious activity may be visible initially but, sooner rather than later, a disaster of titanic proportions was inevitable. It was a scenario just waiting to happen. It begs the question, what do we do when we are holed below the water line?

I's bigger than their stomach

These pretenders were participating at the weekly 'love feast' which was an ideal occasion for informal happy fellowship around a common meal. It was shared by all in the congregation and it was the highlight of their worship together. It was probably the prelude to the Breaking of Bread as reflected by Paul in 1 Corinthians 11:17-34. That was how Tertullian described it in his robust defence of Christianity before the Roman government in AD 197.

It is awfully sad but these wrong-headed participants were making a travesty of the *agapē* meal. They greedily indulged their appetites to the full. They fared sumptuously and had no qualms or reservations about their unrestrained activities. They had no hang-ups as they were only interested in looking after number one!

They threatened the stability and buoyancy of the whole company. It was in serious danger of going under. The peril of running aground was blatantly obvious as time wore on. The false teacher surrounded his error with reams of verbal junk and more than a sprinkling of pseudo piety. All of the time the jagged reef of his doctrinal unreliability was crouching just below the surface.

The tragedy of the early church was that genuine believers in many instances did not recognise these spiritual masqueraders until it was far too late. How many fellowships today, sailing on the ocean of love and harmony, have run aground because false teachers have brought in their wake, division, dissension, and disunity?

The bottom line is, in the words of O S Hawkins, *'they are peace breakers, not peace makers!'*

Empty promises

Jude, in his second analogy, views them as *'clouds without rain'*. What a potent picture that is, especially to the eastern mind. Very often farmers would scan the sky at certain seasons for the appearance of a cloud. In a hot and sticky climate, rain is an essential commodity if you are looking for a prosperous harvest.

When that fleecy cumulus did appear, they rejoiced at the promise and prospect of rain. Nothing could be more unreal and eventually more disappointing than a waterless cloud, it was tenuous and insubstantial. To say the least, it was a monumentally huge let-down.

This was the exact representation of these false teachers. We listen to their preaching but there is nothing to feed on in their words. Richard Baxter said, 'If we can but teach Christ to our people, we teach them all.' These preachers knew little of him!

They claimed to be Bible teachers, but did not teach the Bible.

The appearance is hopeful but the goods are not delivered. It was a classic case of promises, promises, and yet more promises! They were fraudulent. Their productivity was non-existent; in fact, it was virtually nil. All they do is obscure the light.

Fallen on hard times

We need to remember that Jude was largely writing to second generation believers. It was maybe forty years or so after the day of Pentecost, the day the Holy Spirit came and ushered in a brand new era.

Christianity was born in revival!

Thousands upon thousands had been swept into the kingdom of God on a tidal wave of unprecedented blessing. The power of God was unleashed and the whole world was forced to sit up and take notice. For one reason or another, Joe Public was aware of what was happening. The chances are, he could not explain it, nevertheless, he knew something was going on! But, in the second generation, these phenomena had largely disappeared.

Strike when the iron isn't hot

In between the good times and not-so-good times, these emissaries of hell came along and infiltrated the church causing mega-chaos. They assured the people they had answers to the prevailing problems. They offered a host of new ideas along with bigger and better ways of tackling the thorny issues. They promised renewal and a spiritual breakthrough if the congregation pursued a certain course of action.

Jude candidly says they were clouds without water. All talk, no action! They were blown along with the wind. They were fad followers. They are the kind of people who leap on the latest gravy train. They want to investigate everything that is new and conduct a review of anything that is in vogue.

Best served chilled

Martin Luther used to say that *'the one thing the devil cannot stand is ridicule.'*

Jude's estimation of them is less than complimentary. He hands out no floral bouquets or backhanders when he says they are shallow and stupid. From our point of view, we ought to be able to see through them. With all their expertise and professional attempts at public relations, these apostates failed to give much needed refreshment. They were as dry as dust!

Barking up the wrong tree

Jude, in his third sketch, portrays them as *'autumn trees that are without fruit and uprooted'*. He is saying pretty much the same as before – there is appearance without substance – only this time Jude employs a slightly different simile.

It is the insurmountable gap between promise and performance.

Fruit is conspicuous by its absence. There is barrenness and sterility. They are void of any precious life giving sap. They have nothing to give and nothing to show. They have been uprooted because they are useless. The fire was the best place for them.

That, sadly, is the horrendous fate of these artificial believers who lack authenticity. They are not joined to Jesus the Vine and so they will never bloom or blossom in spring. They are dead through and through. There is nothing viable that can be done with them. They are beyond repair and renewal.

Lost forever, forever lost

As if to emphasise their lostness, Jude says they are *'twice dead'*. Their future is horribly certain. They are spiritually dead because they are unrepentant sinners and, because they failed to respond to God's grace, they are destined for an eternity of separation from God, which is the second death. Twice dead because they have only been born once!

S. Maxwell Coder maintains that apostates *'are dead to the fruit of profession and dead to the root of possession.'*

Leftovers

In his fourth comparison, Jude says they are like the *'wild waves of the sea'*. It was the evangelical prophet Isaiah who described the godless as being like the troubled sea (*cf.* Isaiah 57:20, 21).

The sea is never at rest. Its foaming waves incessantly beat upon the shore depositing the flotsam and jetsam which defile the ocean. The beaches are always littered with unsightly and unseemly objects when the frothing spray and spume has subsided. The aftermath is one of filth.

Barclay describes how the waters of the Dead Sea are so impregnated with salt that they strip the bark off driftwood. When such wood is thrown ashore, it gleams bleak and white, more like a pile of dried dead bones than a branch from a living tree.

So it is with the apostate: he makes a mark and he always leaves his mark!

Given time, his real character will be revealed. When the storms of life come and the chilling wind of adversity beats upon his heart, then the real man emerges. Generally speaking, it is not a gratifying or pleasant sight.

A bit of a puke

What lies fermenting on the ocean bed of his innermost being is thrown up in public for all to see. He has exposed himself for what he really is. At the end of it all, as at the beginning, his life is one worthy of a refuse tip. It is rubbish. The problem is, no matter where they go, such men will always get noticed because they leave a mess behind them! A mess, it has to be said, that others have to clear up!

Now you see him, now you don't

And, finally, Jude moves higher to the heavens as he sets before us another snapshot of these pretenders to the throne. They are compared to *'wandering stars'*.

Our present world is one of a family of planets revolving around the sun, lighted by the sun, and controlled by the sun. Sometimes a wandering body from outer space is seen entering the atmosphere, flashing brilliantly for a moment, then either dashing onward in its erratic course into outer space or becoming a dark cinder through friction with the air.

Shooting stars are the epitome of synthetic saints.

They have no real sense of direction and they lack a clear sense of purpose in life. They flicker and sparkle briefly then their scintillating light is momentarily extinguished. They come and they go, here one day, gone the next.

Taken for a ride

These exuberant gentlemen with an overdose of charisma often parade themselves on the evangelical stage in our day. We are bowled over with their brilliance and we are often dazzled (and threatened) by their long list of qualifications and, apparently, excellent credentials. Their CV is that of a high achiever!

These spiritual salesmen are trafficking in divine goods as they offer the latest gimmicks and gadgets to unsuspecting and, sometimes, gullible Christian consumers. The fact is, these apostates are living their lives out of orbit. Often times they are nothing more than a flash in the pan.

Failure is final

It is probably an understatement to say that these men are failures. They failed in the art of living and they fared no better in the art of dying. Throughout their life, they failed miserably in serving. The inescapable fact is, they are failures in eternity!

Charles Swindoll sums them up perfectly when he writes that *'they are as deceptive as hidden reefs, as disappointing as clouds without water, as dead as trees that are without fruit and uprooted, as destructive as wild waves of the sea, and as doomed as falling stars.'*

In reality, they are destined for the *'blackness of darkness'* as Jude so graphically portrays it. What an unthinkable end! These men and women will wander for eternity in a place where light never penetrates. We need to remember that hell is not heaven with the lights switched off! It is a place of loneliness and emptiness. C S Lewis has put it well, 'In hell, everybody will be at an infinite distance from everybody else.'

This is the kernel of Christianity. It is a matter of heaven and hell. If we trust in Jesus as Lord and Saviour, there is a place reserved in heaven for us. If we reject Christ, we take up our reservation in hell. It is as simple as that! As the old Southern Baptist preacher said one day, 'Don't hitch your wagon to a falling star!'

In the words of the eighteenth century evangelist, George Whitefield, 'All talk of hell should be done with a heavy heart and a tear in the eye.'

Hell is a real place. A real place for real people.

Success is ...

I read recently that success is 'being able to hire someone to mow the lawn while you play tennis for exercise.' People who have it made are said to be successful. People who are in the big time are rumoured to be in the same bracket. These are the folk who wear designer label clothes, eat at the best restaurants, and sit in the most expensive seats at the most exclusive social events.

There is more than a grain of truth in the tongue-in-cheek comment of the harassed business entrepreneur, 'The trouble with success is that the formula is the same as the one for a nervous breakdown!'

According to Jude, real success is missing hell! Real success is being ready to die. Real success is being a channel for God in the wider community. It was Hudson Taylor, pioneer missionary to China, who wrote: 'Let there be no reservation. Give yourself up wholly and fully to God whose you are and whom you wish to serve and there can be no disappointment.'

The missionary statesman, C T Studd, who went to the Congo in 1913, captured the mood of the moment when he penned the words, *'Be extravagant for God or the devil, but for God's sake, don't be tepid!'*

8

Cutting the unbiblical cord

'Enoch, the seventh from Adam, prophesied about these men: "See, the Lord is coming with thousands upon thousands of his holy ones to judge everyone, and to convict all the ungodly of all the ungodly acts they have done in the ungodly way, and of all the harsh words ungodly sinners have spoken against him." These men are grumblers and fault-finders; they follow their own evil desires; they boast about themselves and flatter others for their own advantage.'

verses 14-16

You may be surprised (like I was on my first read) to find Enoch's name mentioned a little over halfway through the epistle of Jude. It seems strange! Perhaps, even odd! Actually, it looks a little out of place for he is like a fragrant rose stuck in the middle of prickly thorns.

Beau idéal

Bearing in mind what we looked at in the previous couple of verses, it goes without saying that this man is a gleaming beacon, not a falling star!

To me, Enoch is the quintessential man of God.

He is a wonderful role model for all ages and both sexes. He is exemplary on every front and, in many ways, is everything a believer ought to be. He is a paragon of virtue. I am struggling to think of the name of another Bible character who vies with Enoch inasmuch as he challenges us to a deeper devotional life and stimulates us to enjoy a closer walk with the Lord.

It is quite amazing that in the twelve hundred plus pages of Scripture Enoch is rarely mentioned at all! All his remarkable achievements under God are compressed and compacted neatly into a sparse handful of verses. We can count them on ten fingers!

Enoch was not ...

- the founding father of a nation like Abraham,
- a charismatic leader like Moses,
- a conquering warrior like Gideon,
- an eminent statesman like Daniel.

From reading between the lines it appears that the untarnished Enoch was a very ordinary individual whose heart God had touched. He was a country bumpkin whose life the Lord had graciously transformed. Yet, alongside Noah, he shares the honourable distinction of being a man of whom it was said, 'he walked with God'.

Roots

Enoch is identified in verse 14 as *'the seventh from Adam'*. The seven names are listed in Genesis 5:1-18 as:

> Adam,
> > Seth,
> > > Enosh,
> > > > Kenan,
> > > > > Mahalaleel,
> > > > > > Jared,
> > > > > > > Enoch.

The reason why is fairly obvious. Enoch was from the godly line of Adam and, for that reason, must not be confused with his worldly-wise namesake who came from the secondary line of Cain (*cf.* Genesis 4:17).

Enoch is a different branch in the family tree.

It is worth noting that the writer to the Hebrews ignores the first Enoch in history. When he was looking for someone of real significance to slot into Hebrews 11 as an example of faith,

* he passed over Jabal, a top agriculturist of his day, and
* Jubal, a prime mover and shaker in the aesthetic fields of music and entertainment, and
* Tubal-Cain, a magnate in manufacturing (*cf.* Genesis 4:20-22).

Enoch was not a dazzling figure in world history. He did not live in the public eye. He did not have a high profile. He was not a great leader and personality of the day. We are not told that he pleased his friends or family. He may not have been as well off because of his faith, but God told him that he was well pleased with him and elevated him to a place of recognition.

What a difference in two men with the same name!

What's in a name?

It is interesting to observe the significance of the names given to Enoch's father and grandfather. For example, the almost unpronounceable name of his grandfather, Mahalaleel, means 'splendour or praise of God'. The underlying thought is of someone who is enthralled with the grandeur and glory of God and who, at the same time, is intrinsically aware of the awesomeness of Jehovah.

There is no big deal about his father's name. To an etymological purist, it is actually quite boring, it simply means 'descendant'. It is not unreasonable to assume that Jared did not follow fully in his father's footsteps but was more conscious of man and his abilities. Like father, like son, does not seem appropriate in this instance. It is a classic case of where the emphasis is placed on the human plane!

Enoch's name means 'dedicated'. There is no question about it, he certainly lived up to his name. He is a remarkable example of a God-centred, God-controlled life.

Tough times

The day in which Enoch lived was characterised by a rapid advance in civilisation, art, and science. We know from Genesis 4:16-22 that the world of that day was fashioned by the sons of Cain. You name it, they did it! The fact is, that pre-Flood civilisation was possibly as splendid as Greece or Rome. Cultured? Yes! But the first poetry written was on the subject of murder (*cf.* Genesis 4:23, 24). Sadly, it was just as godless!

Life for Enoch was far from easy. It was uphill all the way! He lived and worked in dark and difficult times. It was an age when sin abounded and moral principles were deliberately swept aside.

Enoch was an integral part of the antediluvian civilisation which felt the repercussions of Adam's sin. In the third millennium, we continue to experience the fallout from one man's fateful decision.

The caption over his era is found in Genesis 6:5 where we read concerning man that 'every inclination of the thoughts of his heart was only evil all the time'. Times were bad! However, in the midst of such evil and reprobate behaviour, Enoch continued to walk closely with the Lord and he bore a silent testimony to his God.

Changing nappies at 65!

God blessed Enoch when, at the age of 65, his wife presented him with his firstborn son. Needless to say, Enoch was over the moon! He was cock-a-hoop and delirious with joy! Can you imagine it? He is changing diapers for the first time in his life! For Enoch, that was par for the course, he just had to smile and get on with it!

Selecting a name for the new baby was no problem either! Earlier God had given Enoch a revelation that, when his son would die, every living creature upon the earth would be destroyed by a universal flood. That is why he called him Methuselah for his name means 'when he is dead, it shall be sent'.

New man on the block

It seems to me that something enormously significant happened at this point in Enoch's life. The birth of his son triggered a spiritual sensor in his heart which resulted in him coming into a more meaningful relationship with the Lord. Life changing events are often used by the Lord to bring us to our knees and keep us on our toes! And for the best part of three centuries afterwards, Enoch walked in happy fellowship with his God.

Mind you, he was probably ostracised by those in the community as they reckoned he was some kind of religious oddball. He was dubbed a monomaniacal fanatic. I am sure he was the butt of much ridicule and, no doubt, mean individuals would have made him the lead character in their smutty smear stories.

His was an extraordinarily lonely path and, on more than one occasion, it exposed his high level of vulnerability. But, Enoch being Enoch, did not let that deter him. He just kept on going for God was with him. That made all the difference!

Missing, believed ...

One day, totally out of the blue, Enoch's assured confidence and implicit trust in God were amply rewarded when he was ushered into the immediate presence of his God without experiencing death. He escaped it! Having said that, he did not feel as if he had missed out in any way! That was the surreal moment when faith gave way to sight and promise turned into sweet reality.

The patriarchal funeral bell tolled ominously and often in Genesis 5. That chapter has been aptly called the epitaph chapter of the Bible for it contains the phrase 'and he died' many times. Not for Enoch, however. He was different. What happened to him had never happened to anyone else! This was a first! Enoch left this world not by the dark tunnel of death but by the golden bridge of translation. His was a royal entrance into the eternal home of God.

For Enoch, it was merely a change of location, not a change of company.

G. Campbell Morgan illustrates it beautifully when he says, 'Enoch was a wonderful man who used to go for long walks with God. How did it end? One day they walked on and on and when they had gone so far, God turned and said to him, "Enoch, you're a long way from home, you'd better come in and stay with me!'"

Unwittingly, Enoch became forever a picture of what death is to the Christian – only an incident, hardly worth mentioning. That is the reality that Enoch pioneered by faith.

A lonely voice

Enoch was a prophet before the Flood.

His was a two pronged, double-barrelled message:

* Jesus is coming, and
* judgment is coming.

With such a twin thrust to his prophecy, Enoch did not mince his words. He did not need to because he knew God would sort everything and everyone out in his own time. It is obvious that he and Jude are singing from the same song sheet for that is what Jude believed. Hence his open letter to the churches.

Attention, please

His first word *'see'* (Greek, *idou*) is a lion-hearted attempt to get others to listen carefully as something important is about to follow. He pleads for their undivided attention as he divulges a vital piece of information to them. In the next breath, he heralded forth with clarity and earnest conviction the message of the second advent of Jesus Christ.

He preached about the coming again of the Lord Jesus with immense enthusiasm.

Is it any wonder he said *'see'* for this is the backbone of his message. It adds a new dimension to it. It gives it a sharp cutting edge. It gives him fresh impetus as he attacks these shameless teachers. The foolish activities of these faith sharks was subversive.

With this great assurance burning in his soul, he fearlessly denounced and forthrightly condemned these ambassadors of the devil. Jude was resolute and unflinching in his stand for purity of fellowship and doctrine because he knew Christ was returning. But he does not stop there. There are no half measures with Jude!

The Lord is coming!

Jude proceeds to show the reason why Jesus is coming and with whom he is coming. When the signal is given for Jesus to break through the clouds, the great news is, he will not be alone for he will be accompanied in regal splendour with *'thousands upon thousands of his holy ones'*. Oh yes, the angels will be at his side but so too will his believing people.

It will be a heart-stopping scene of magnificence and majesty as the Lord Jesus returns to planet earth.

This has all to do with bringing to fruition the blessed hope of the people of God. One day the heavens will glow with splendour and every eye will be fixed on the sky. All over the world – men, women, boys, and girls – will behold the undiluted and unrivalled wonder of the King of kings returning.

In that day, the Lord will be admired and glorified in his saints and, in tandem, hardened sinners will recognise and confess that Jesus is Lord. So too will the synthetic saints! It is to deal with them and their companions that Christ has come.

After the Lord's feet touch down on the Mount of Olives, he will swiftly inaugurate his policy of firm and fair retribution when justice will be seen to be done. He is coming as Judge and, in that capacity, he will pass a custodial sentence on those who have withstood his gracious overtures. Thank God, that is the day when error will be vanquished by truth.

One, two, three, four

In verse 15, the word *'ungodly'* is sonorously repeated four times, like driving nails in their coffin. That is what Jude thinks of these apostates. Basically, God did not figure in their plans and, in an act of defiance, they left him out of their calculations. They are bereft of any sense of awe and reverence towards him. Their lives are impoverished and destitute as they have lived a lie. In the final analysis, they only fooled themselves. Clearly, then, this word sums them up with devastating laser-like accuracy.

Open mouth, enter feet

The *'harsh words'* these *'ungodly sinners have spoken against him'* is an expression used by Jude which is indicative of all the blasphemous propaganda that flowed from their lips with apparent fluency and relative ease. They became victims of their own verbosity.

They are sinners in the dock. At the bar of God, their sensuous deeds and brazen disregard for biblical standards testified against them. Their works and impropriety spoke out loudly against them as they froze on the spot. They fabricated a God who was not in the least concerned about Christian lifestyle and now they have been caught out! They cannot pull the wool over his eyes nor can they hide from his all-seeing eye.

They talked themselves into it. Now they cannot talk their way out of it.

It is much too late for that kind of thing. By then, the tables will have turned.

The ball is fairly and squarely in their court when they stand before the Lord at the great white throne (*cf.* Revelation 20:11-15). They will know all about it for they will be on the receiving end and, to make matters infinitely worse, they have no defence, they have no leg to stand on, there is no plea bargaining, they have no right of appeal, and their destiny is sealed and settled before a Judge with no jury!

God's strange work

I think it is immensely helpful for us to realise that, at the end of time, God's judgment is threefold in nature.

* It is *personal,*
* *purposeful,* and
* *perfect.*

You see, judgment is not an event which may or may not happen. When we look at history through the spectacles of Scripture, we see that God has done it before, many times before, and from verse 15, it is abundantly clear that he will do it again!

Sometimes we tend to forget that the last chapter has not yet been written in the book of their lives. These false teachers as well as every sinner on planet earth are guilty of cosmic high treason for they live without giving God his rightful place in their lives! The simple fact remains that God has not forgotten!

A fifth column

Reaching an emotional climax in verse 16, we discover a number of identification marks on these false teachers. In fact, Jude is unbelievably specific, we cannot miss what he is saying and hit the wall! He describes these religious rogues in enough detail to make them blush!

Jude has made it clear and plain in the course of his remarks that lawlessness is the hallmark of these synthetic saints and what we have here simply confirms that prognosis. This weird evil of rebellion stems from the fact that they have no respect for God or any form of structured human authority.

These saboteurs are guilty of spiritual terrorism. They are engaged in guerrilla warfare in the local church and, in that role, they are rightly portrayed as the godfathers of religious violence.

On the grumble trail

For starters, Jude describes these die-hards as *'grumblers'*. That is an easily recognisable trait in their crooked character. It seems to me that grumblers are always a nuisance. They are a perpetual pain in the neck! These folk are constantly backbiting against those who preach the truth, not unlike Israel against Moses.

After Israel had crossed the Red Sea and seen the Egyptian taskforce destroyed, only three days elapsed before trouble erupted over the lack of potable water. We read in Exodus 15:24 that 'the people grumbled against Moses, saying, "What are we to drink?"'

Believe it or not, it took less than 72 hours for miffed resentment to set in!

Shortly after this, the lack of decent drinking water was evidently becoming a sore point for them. When they trekked as far as Rephidim, their blood is boiling for we read in Exodus 17:3 that 'the people were thirsty for water there, and they grumbled against Moses. They said, "Why did you bring us up out of Egypt to make us and our children and livestock die of thirst?"' It is a sad state of affairs, isn't it! People have very short memories and it does not take much for them to start on the grumble trail.

Incidentally, this is the only time this particular word, *gongustēs*, appears in the entire New Testament. It is one of those splendidly onomatopoeic words. It means 'someone who harps on about an issue and does not know when to keep quiet'. It typifies the person who has a bee in their bonnet and who will not rest until they have aired their point of view. They are bellyachers! In the original language, it carried the idea of the cooing of doves. Well, these infidels were certainly not bird mouthed.

'Our grumbling is the devil's music!' (Thomas Watson)

It is not a loud outspoken dissatisfaction. On the contrary, it is a constant undercurrent of incessant muttering below the breath. The person may not be clearly heard, or readily understood, but they have succeeded in registering a protest. It is a classic case of verbal rumbling. It is not unlike a volcano making unwelcome and intrusive noises in the background. This attitude betrays a spirit of acrimony and it shows itself when they engage in a whispering campaign against the leadership.

Their murmuring involved three basic denials:

* they deplored the *providence* of God,
* they despised the *provision* of God, and
* they denounced the *person* of God.

Nit pickers!

However, Jude does not stop there, he goes a step further when he labels them *'fault finders'*. I think it is interesting to note that Jude's second word picture, *mempsimoiros*, is not an Old Testament one. It is one that comes from among the stock characters of the situation comedies of his day, like Andy Capp in the *Daily Mirror*.

It is the moaner who is never satisfied with his lot. In summer, they wish it was winter, and in winter, they wish it was summer. These are the malcontents! They have the unenviable knack of complaining and saying the wrong thing at the right time. You see, one always leads to the other! Nothing was ever right. They search out and focus on the things that are lacking in a church.

The fact is, no local church is perfect this side of heaven. We all recognise there are areas of our church life which could well be improved and, with God's help, we should set the wheels in motion to reach that goal. But, no matter what was good, bad, or indifferent in the church, these folk found fault with it.

They were a miserable bunch. They were unhappy with their lot in life and they projected their pent up feelings on those in the congregation. Nothing measured up to their high standards. They were always poking holes.

Theirs was a ministry of pulling down, rather than building up.

No matter what it was, it proved to be a perennial bone of contention. For them, the grass was always greener on the other side!

We could describe these men as the liberal theologians of the early church. They were the modernists of Jude's day. They wanted to adopt a different approach to the word of God and advised others to give more credence to the traditions of men.

It seems to me that these guys were kamikaze in their outlook. Relentlessly, they waged a battle against all and sundry as they gradually undermined the very foundation of not a few. Slowly but surely they were pulling the carpet from under the feet of the average church member.

Men behaving badly

The third numbing characteristic of these apostates is their natural inkling to *'follow their own evil desires'*. In doing this, they have a hidden agenda! At the end of the day, they want to use the church as a vehicle for their own egos. Basically, it boils down to them being slaves to their own sin. It is the 'I'm alright, Jack' attitude of blatant self-centredness.

The expression Jude employs here is not only a lust for sexual gratification, it can also refer to the passionate craving for some other object of good or evil intent. By and large, their activity was geared not to the spiritual part of man's makeup but to his carnal and fleshly appetite.

They were not acting on impulse. Neither were they acting on the spur of the moment. Nor were they perpetrating their acts of pointless violence only when a tingling feeling was felt at the base of their spine. Their behaviour was planned and premeditated. Their strategy was mapped out and their goals clearly defined. Their one value is pleasure and their one dynamic is desire.

Their outlook was libertine. Their policy was hedged in antinomian phraseology. They were freedom fighters and, in their own eyes, the end justified the means. Deluded, they most certainly were. In a nutshell, these men are going back on their initial commitment to Christ.

Big heads!

These false teachers were stoned drunk with an inflated feeling of their own self-importance. Jude says in the same verse that they spend their time *'boasting about themselves'*. It is the empty can that makes the most noise!

They were loud mouthed and big mouthed!

They were famed for their notoriety. They were double talkers both in private and in public and, when all was said and done, it was nothing more than pedantic palaver. It was a load of flowery drivel which, in the words of Shakespeare, is 'full of sound and fury, signifying nothing'. They had swallowed the famous Blarney Stone! Whether seated in a room or standing at a rostrum, they would soon win an argument and woo yet another unsuspecting individual.

These sneaky false teachers were devious through and through. They showed utter contempt and scorn as they attacked the mind and intelligence of others around them. They said things simply to twist unwary people around their little finger and get them going in their direction.

It is fairly obvious they were conceited and, consequently, acted in a high-handed manner. They were audacious and pompous in their dealings with ordinary people. They could never be pinned down on any aspect of truth because of their profoundly arrogant style and their innate ability to sidestep and dodge controversy.

Sometimes they were like a babbling brook, at other times they were like a river bursting its banks.

Flattery gets you …

The final distinguishing trademark of these merchandisers of error is recorded by Jude as their inherent ability to steal the show by *'flattering others for their own advantage'*. Flattery devalues people. It has turned more heads than garlic! Benjamin Disraeli coined the phrase, 'Talk to a man about himself and he will listen to you for hours!'

Flattery has been defined as *'the art of one person telling another person what he or she already thinks about themselves!'*

Christopher Green, writing in *The Bible Speaks Today* commentary says, 'A flatterer has precisely the same evaluation of our talents and abilities that we have always secretly felt, he understands our motivations and puts them into words that we would never dare to utter, he promises a future that is centred around the very achievements we have always fantasised about.' That is flattery, pure and simple.

Be alert!

I think most of us are alert to the dangers of flattery, but we need to wake up to the fact that the reality can be very difficult to disentangle and escape from. It is the devil's net and we need to be careful lest we fall into it.

You see, their outlook in life revolved around me, myself, and I. They were in it for what they could get out of it. They were self-centred as they continually looked after 'number one'. They were intoxicated with their own personality cult.

There are two types of people in today's church:

• those who enter a room announcing, 'Well, here I am!' *and*
• those who go in and say, 'Ah, there you are!'

You do not need to be a rocket scientist to suss out which group these folk were in! They had been given a foothold and it was not long until they established themselves at the control panel. In all innocence, they were given an inch but they were not content until they had taken a mile, or two.

The fact of the matter is, these folk are into empire building in a big way.

When we are faced with that type of scenario, our response must be quick and ruthlessly efficient. It calls for drastic measures. Realistically, it is them or us! If we are going to survive, we have no viable alternative but to cut off their oxygen supply at source.

9

The religious bourgeoisie

'But, dear friends, remember what the apostles of our Lord Jesus Christ foretold. They said to you, "In the last times there will be scoffers who will follow their own ungodly desires." These are the men who divide you, who follow mere natural instincts and do not have the Spirit.'

verses 17-19

Green shoots of recovery

The opening word *'but'* in verse 17 would seem to indicate that the first gleams of dawn are breaking through the gloom. There is a light at the end of the tunnel. It is as if Jude breathes a huge sigh of relief in the text. It is only one word but that one word says it all.

It signals a reversal. The church can make its presence felt in the world. It can impact its day, it can influence its generation, and it can effectively deal with these charlatans.

The original Greek word conveys the idea of *'but, as for you'*. I think the contrast which Jude makes between real believers and these cosmetic Christians is quite incredible. There is a vast gulf that cannot be spanned between truth and error. They are poles apart.

No chip on his shoulder

Again, Jude refers to the saints as *'dear friends'*.

They were his dear friends because they were God's dear friends!

He definitely cannot say that about the opposition. It is an open display of warmth and affection as he tries to reassure them that they are still very much upon his heart. His opinion of them is unchanged even though they have been dragged through a thorny hedge backwards.

Perhaps they were tempted to think that Jude was alone in his thinking and in his appraisal of their situation. The chances are that some of them felt he had an axe to grind. Maybe they thought he had it in for them for one reason or another. Some of them probably believed he was over-reacting to the present climate in their Christian fellowships. Rightly or wrongly, a number of them may have assumed that Jude was swinging the pendulum to the opposite extreme.

But, to be fair to Jude, he was not. Their spiritual forefathers said this would happen. Their one-time contemporaries had warned of something similar. The way forward for them was not to adopt some new innovation but to rediscover what had been previously revealed.

O S Hawkins reminds us, *'The truth is, if the words are new, they are not true.'*

A quote a day keeps the devil at bay

Jude's rock-solid word of exhortation to these beleaguered believers revolves around the word *'remember'*. Actually, this word *mimnēskō* is the first imperative verb in the book of Jude, and an imperative is a command. The all-important question is: remember what? The words of the other apostles! Namely, the likes of Paul, Peter, and John. They all mentioned it, more than once, I hasten to add!

- In Paul's impassioned farewell speech to the church at Ephesus, he said, 'I know that after I leave, savage wolves will come in among you and will not spare the flock' (Acts 20:29).
- To Timothy, his son in the gospel ministry, Paul wrote, 'The Spirit clearly says that in later times some will abandon the faith and follow deceiving spirits and things taught by demons' (1 Timothy 4:1).
- Peter, the big fisherman-cum-apostle, penned these words, 'First of all,

you must understand that in the last days scoffers will come, scoffing and following their own evil desires' (2 Peter 3:3).
- John was batting from the same crease when he said, 'Many deceivers, who do not acknowledge Jesus Christ as coming in the flesh, have gone out into the world. Any such person is the deceiver and the antichrist' (2 John 7).

We should remember the wise words of George Santayana, the Spanish philosopher, 'He who forgets the past is condemned to repeat it.' Jude was sincerely hoping and praying that they would be able to recall these quotations, and a host of others. They could not afford to neglect these pertinent warnings. It was a classic case of do or die. If they failed to get their act together, the consequences would be serious and catastrophic for the local testimony; in no time at all, it would become a centre for false religion and the light would be extinguished.

The apostles hit the nail on the head and, if the early church failed to listen, they would take a hammering from the devil in the guise of these factious saints. Whether they realised it or not, their boat was being rocked with a tidal wave of erroneous doctrine and a lot of shilly-shallying in matters of faith and practice.

If only ...

What caused Jude more heartache than anything else is that this situation need not have arisen in the first place. As we have noted, they had been well warned. Jude piles the pressure on for he tells them that the apostles in the first century had a message foretelling what was going to happen. It was a prophetic utterance and, as we can expect from an authentic voice, their prediction came true.

For quite some time, the danger lights were flashing red. The alarm bells were ringing!

This round of trouble could so easily have been averted and avoided if only they had listened and paid rapt attention to the servants of the Lord.

Never mind the apostles, if these folk lived within striking distance of Jerusalem, a continuous traffic of gifted Christian speakers would have passed through to speak at their meetings. As Christopher Green indicates, 'Jude calls them to remember the constant refrain of their messages, rather than to recall one particularly hard-hitting talk: the verb for *'said'* is in the imperfect tense, and means "they were in the habit of saying to you."'

Playful protagonists

Jude proceeds to reinforce his argument by reminding them of the apostles' warning and description of these tyrants in their midst. He calls them *'scoffers'*. The Greek word *empaiktēs* implies 'to act in a childish fashion, to be childish, to play, and to jest'. That is where they really excelled themselves!

They lack maturity. They are the ones who despise religion and laugh at morality. They live loose lifestyles and make the faith a subject of irreverent humour. In 2 Peter 3:3, the term seems to refer to more secular people who deride religion in the name of rationalism.

They are seen as having a view of world history which excludes the supernatural and as those who pour cold water on the idea of Christ's return.

These are the people who know not when and where to draw the line. They always go over the top. Life is treated as one big joke. They lived and worked as if they were answerable to nobody. They were responsible alone for their irresponsible actions. In reality, no-one could work with them.

The most protruding feature in their personality is that *'they follow their own ungodly desires'*. From Jude's perspective, it really sticks out a mile. They are prisoners to their own perversity and are in bondage to their own badness.

Twisted theology

The challenge comes when they attempt to justify their behaviour from the word of God.

It is one thing to fall in love with Jesus, but we cannot fall in love with Jesus without falling in line with Jesus!

Such folk are happy to persist in going their own way and, at the same time, they are keen to support their lifestyle by ramming a plethora of Bible verses down your throat. The fact that someone has a theology, and is able to justify his position by quoting Bible verses, is no guarantee that he is being totally honest with himself in his thinking.

When we come to verse 19, we discover that Jude is now tying up the loose ends in his argument against these dangerous false teachers who pose as half-baked saints. He labels them for what they are as he tells it like it is.

Church splitters

We glean that from Jude's qualified use of the word *'divide'*. The word *apodiorizo* translated *'divide'* occurs only once in Greek literature in a passage used by Aristotle in the sense of 'to separate or to make a distinction'. In other words, to put it bluntly, these false teachers cause division and discord. They throw a large spanner in the works. They toss a cat among the pigeons!

They were bringing division where in fact there should not be division. They were causing havoc and chaos where the people should be moving together as one in the Lord. They make factions in the fellowship. They disrupt the life of the local congregation and bring disunity among the members. They are guilty of exclusivism. Instead of drawing a circle to take men in, they drew a circle to shut men out!

Wherever they go, these men leave a litany of fractured relationships and shattered dreams behind them. Friendships falter, strife surfaces, and congregations crumble. In a word, they are troublemakers!

Driving a wedge

Apostates are set before us as those *'who follow mere natural instincts'*. We have this thought brought out earlier in the epistle as Jude reminds us forcefully of their self-seeking ambition (*cf.* verses 4, 10). It smacks of people who are less than fully human.

The Gnostics had formulated their own theory about man. They reasoned that not all men have spirit (pneuma), the ability to think. They stated that all mankind have body and breath (psyche), but not spirit. Therefore, the fact that a man may have physical life does not mean that he can think! In other words, some men do not differ from animals, they are just flesh and blood. Other men, an elite class, had secret wisdom and special insights on life.

Jude's comment about them is a big put-down. These animal-like apostates polarise the church community by adopting a sectarian spirit. They were earthbound in their thinking and worldly minded in their outlook. There is nothing about them that is spiritual.

Jude's use of the word *'natural'* is fascinating. It is the word *psuchikos* from which we derive the English word 'psychological'.

They know how to use psychology in an attempt to win others, while at the same time, theirs is only a psychological experience.

The missing piece

Jude reminds us that they *'do not have the Spirit'*. In other words, they were devoid of the Holy Spirit of God in their lives. He was not alive in their hearts. They know nothing of the power of God in their lives. They had never experienced anything of the ministry of the Holy Spirit within them or upon them. He was completely foreign to them.

This is the decisive note in Jude's description and it clinches the argument. Because the Holy Spirit is not in residence in their lives, it means they are not an integral part of the global family of God. Jude makes it abundantly clear that they are not even Christians. They are still sinners. Paul was on the same wavelength when he wrote, 'If anyone does not have the Spirit of Christ, he does not belong to Christ' (Romans 8:9).

A Christian is someone who is:

- *baptised* by the Holy Spirit (1 Corinthians 12:13),
- *sealed* by the Holy Spirit (Ephesians 1:13),
- *indwelt* by the Holy Spirit (John 14:17),
- *taught* by the Holy Spirit (John 16:13),
- *led* by the Holy Spirit (Romans 8:14), and
- *filled* with the Holy Spirit (Ephesians 5:18).

If there were any questions lurking in the back of our minds as to whether an apostate is a lost soul or merely a Christian who is mistaken in some of his ideas, this certainly settles it, once and for all.

An apostate is an unregenerate person.

He lacks the distinguishing mark of the true believer. The divine imprimatur is not graven on his heart. That is tough, sock-it-to-them talking from Jude.

A life-size image

When we take a step back and carefully look at a full view of the portrait Jude has sketched, we see:

- lips sneering contemptuously in complaint,
- a faultfinding finger pointing in ridicule,
- eyes glinting with lust,
- an eyebrow lifted in arrogance,
- the appearance of a flatterer who loves to manipulate others.

On a personal level, I find it rather grotesque and repulsive. At least, we know what to look for and we know what to listen for.

The evangelical church, especially in the West, is passing through challenging times. We see things which are so markedly similar to those Jude has described that we find it difficult not to think that somehow he had taken a trip forward in time to the twenty-first century.

If Jude were here, he would say, *'I told you so!'*

10

Fighting the spiritual flab

'But you, dear friends, build yourselves up in your most holy faith and pray in the Holy Spirit.'

verse 20

'Who are you?'

The park keeper's question cracked like a rifle shot across Frankfurt's Tiergarten jolting back to some kind of reality the ragged figure slouched untidily on a bench. Slowly, he raised his head, looked forlornly at the official, and said, *'I wish I knew!'*

Arthur Schopenhauer, one of his country's greatest philosophers, had spent years wrestling with the insoluble problems of the universe and of man's existence on earth, but he had no clear picture of his own identity. Needless to say, the whole of his life was impoverished as a result.

Finding our identity in Christ

Jude says in a lovely turn of phrase: *'but you, dear friends'.* How uplifting and encouraging are these words! The contrast between what has gone before in the previous few verses and what is happening now is glaringly obvious. We have moved from a cesspool into a beautiful garden!

As it were, Jude draws a line in the sand. The thought behind Jude's deliberate choice of phrase is to heavily underline the fact that they were saints.

Sometimes we are inclined to think that a saint is a particularly good Christian who really loves the Lord more than we do. We set them on a pedestal and we view them as a kind of honours graduate in Christian living. That is an awful pity for that is not how the New Testament shows them.

We are saints and *'dear friends'* because we have been brought into a personal relationship with the Lord Jesus. Jude is quietly reassuring them when he says, 'you really are dear friends, friends of mine, and friends of God.'

- At times, they may not *feel* like it, but they are!
- At times, they may not *act* like it, but they are!
- At times, they may not *look* like it, but they are!

This is a fact that cannot be stressed often enough. No-one can ride roughshod over them. They belong to God.

The great news is, we stand arm-in-arm with them as members of *'the Church of Jesus Christ of present day saints!'*

Where the rubber hits the road

Having reminded them of who they are, Jude says, be what you are. And the way to do that is found in the rest of verse 20, and on into verse 21. In a series of four pieces of pastoral wisdom which are designed to be an effective remedy against spiritual danger, Jude urges us to keep a watch on ourselves, and on one another. He tells us:

- what we ought to be doing for ourselves (verses 20, 21), and
- what we ought to be doing for others (verses 22, 23).

God designed men and women to be doers, he made us to be active. We live in an age in which we are encouraged to sit back and watch other people perform, but that is not what we are here for. The fact remains, Christianity is not a spectator sport! The stirring challenge to the church of the first millennium was: if you want to keep your head above water, do what I am telling you to do! That advice is just as appropriate for today's church in the third millennium.

No pain, no gain

This structured syllabus would enable them to survive in the midst of such debilitating and trying circumstances. When others were going down and under, they would be able to walk tall with their faith rooted and fixed in God. This was the way forward. If the truth be told, this was the only way forward.

There were no short cuts and no quick fixes. There was no easy road to success. It would involve sheer hard graft and consolidated effort on their part but, at the end of the day, it would prove to be eminently worthwhile. There will obviously be short-term advantages by avidly pursuing such a curriculum. However, the maximum benefit will only be derived in the longer term. Jude is not thinking about today or tomorrow, it is the day after which is uppermost in his mind.

Four into one do go

There are four facets to this ongoing programme which Jude so skilfully outlines for them. They should be taken together as a corporate entity and not hatched off singly or separately. The four of them are intertwined and each one is interlinked. One will automatically lead to the other thereby ensuring continuity and a measure of consistency in our spiritual growth and development.

If we follow Jude's advice to the letter, we will not become lopsided in our striving after maturity. There will be a balance to our walk with the Lord. The four verbs are *'build, pray, keep, and wait'*.

... the builder!

Jude's first word of exhortation is to *'build yourselves up in your most holy faith'*. Here is practical theology at its finest and best. Here is the Christian dressed in his working clothes. This is a do-it-yourself study module. It is a piece of sound and sensible advice imploring us to get our act together.

Jude is not thinking here of their personal faith in Jesus. Rather, he is reverting back to what he spoke of much earlier in his epistle when he drew attention in verse 3 to *'the faith once delivered to the saints'*. It is the written word of God. That is what he is focusing on.

It is the truth of God, penned by men of God, under the control and illumination of the Spirit of God, for all the people of God.

The 'holy' Bible

With characteristic flair, Jude describes the faith as being *'most holy'*. It suggests the sacred nature of such a revelation. It is out of this world in that it is heavenly in origin and divine in essence. This truth has not been thought up by a handful of people sitting in a committee room in some mission headquarters, it has come from God. It is the good news that the holy God has revealed and made known to man. It is something which we could never have found out for ourselves, nor could the brightest brains in the world have done so. It has come from heaven.

The other side of the coin tells me that it is *'holy'* because it has a profound influence on our hearts and minds. When we respond to it, it makes us holy.

Be insulated!

Probably the best way to protect ourselves against false teaching is to familiarise ourselves with the truth of Scripture. There is no better way. If we want to be inoculated against the persuasive charm of the apostate then we need to be indoctrinated with the word of God.

In a crazy old world, the word of God is sure and steadfast. It proves to be an anchor for the soul of man in the many storms of life. When the sands of time are shifting and sinking, we have something we can grasp on to and something we can hold on to.

Come what may, the Faith will always remain intact and unaffected by the chilling winds of liberal theology and the howling storms of apostasy. The word of God stands unmoved amidst the gales of Higher Criticism that have been levelled against it. Look, there is not even the slightest trace of a crack nor is there any sign of strain being imposed on the infrastructure. Today it towers o'er the many wrecks of time.

What's his is mine

Did you notice how personal it all is? Jude says it is *'your most holy faith'*. Oh yes, it is God's word, and in that special sense it belongs to him. But, when we are brought into a saving relationship with Jesus, that which is his automatically becomes ours.

The word *'your'* is inextricably linked with the word *'yourselves'* in that here is something for us to do. We are meant to be proactive as the people of God. Jude wants to see the whole of our lives – that is, our intellects, actions, consciences, motives, and imaginations – brought increasingly into conformity to God's word.

We have a solemn responsibility to spend time with the word, and around the word, in private, as well as in our regular attendance at the house of God. What we hear from other gifted expositors should only supplement our own diet.

Couch potato Christians

From observation, it seems to me that it is much easier to be a spiritual sponge than it is to be a serious student of the word of God. The members of the Chinese church used to have a saying, 'No Bible – no breakfast!' If we followed that motto, I wonder how many of us would go hungry. How many there are who prefer to soak everything up that they hear from the pulpit and neglect their personal quiet time.

R C Sproul comments, 'We fail in our duty to study God's word not so much because it is difficult to understand. Not so much because it is dull and boring. But because it is work. Our problem is not a lack of intelligence or a lack of passion. Our problem is that we are lazy.'

The majority of believers that I know prefer to be spoon fed and treated as babes in a nursery environment instead of making an earnest effort and getting into the Bible themselves.

Jude is talking here about building. The word is in the present tense which implies it is an ongoing occupation. It is a life-long activity. The bottom line is that the more we put into it, the more we will get out of it. It will take lots of determination, dedication, and discipline.

- We *study* it,
- we *believe* it,
- we *apply* it, and
- we *obey* it!

Toning up

The milk and meat of the word are provided so that we might progress down the road to maturity in Christ. Studying the Bible is comparable to spiritual weight lifting. It makes us stronger and stronger, so we can stand firmly in the place of blessing and not be dragged or pushed out of it. We will develop spiritual muscle and that is tremendous; at the same time, though, we need to keep ourselves in excellent shape. We need to tone up daily as we diligently exercise our minds and hearts before an open book.

On a spiritual level, faith and flab are not compatible!

Jude is more or less saying: *'build yourself up in your most holy faith'* for that is your personal responsibility before the Lord. He says, I cannot do it for you, only you can do something about it!

A safety net

Having said that, there is a lot more to it than meets the eye! It is not only something we are meant to do on our own in a solo effort. We need to recognise that we are in it together in the family of God. The word *'yourselves'* is a plural which indicates a common concern and love, it is a corporate activity.

Yes, Jude says, do it yourself, but do not neglect quality time with others in the church family, we are meant to grow together into the likeness of Christ. There is a grave danger in operating on our own for we become easy meat for the enemy and we become like sitting ducks for the apostate. We can support each other when we share and study together around the open word of God.

The fact is, a brick cannot be cemented into a building unless it is on the building site!

Talking about prayer

The second guideline Jude gives is to *'pray in the Holy Spirit'*. When we read the word, God communicates with us. When we engage in prayer, we are communing with God. When God speaks to us, we respond by talking things over with him. The Bible without prayer has no dynamic, prayer without the Bible has no direction.

It dawned on me recently that those men and women in the Bible who were mighty prayer warriors never read a book on prayer nor attended a seminar on prayer. They just prayed!

Prayer is something we talk so much about, but rarely do!

We read a lot of best-selling books, we listen to a lot of audio tapes, we buy fast-moving videos from keynote conference speakers, we attend many unforgettable high-pitched seminars – all on prayer!

It seems to me from where I stand that we know a lot more about prayer in our minds than we may have actually experienced in our hearts. Someone has said and I tend to agree with them that 'people who do not pray are practical atheists, no matter what they call themselves; and churches that do not pray are secular organisations, no matter what is stated in their doctrinal basis.'

The funny side of prayer

Some prayers amaze me, others simply amuse me!

The chances are, we often say our prayers, but do we really pray? I may have perfect diction, beautiful phraseology, and wonderful grammar, but that is not prayer. I can repeat, 'Lord bless me and my wife, son John and his wife, us four and no more!' every morning and evening, but that is not prayer.

When we sit down and analyse our prayers, how feeble and weak our efforts really are. I am honestly convinced that many of our prayers contain more nonsense than sense! We employ our pet phrases and regularly use the well-worn clichés. Some believers I know even adopt a rather unusual tone of voice when praying in public.

If some of the folk who pray in our churches were really talking to God, I cannot for the life of me see how our heavenly Father could have been favourably impressed with their apparent inability to hold an intelligent conversation.

It must be a frustrating experience for the Lord to listen to millions of prayers that say nothing, ask nothing, and expect nothing!

I am reminded of a story about an author who desperately needed some hard currency. He wired his publisher: 'How much advance will you pay for my latest novel of fifty thousand words?' The publisher replied, 'How important are the words?' I like that!

Some of the words that make up our prayers are not very important. Let me show you what I mean from a couple of stories I read recently.

• During a series of ministry meetings in a southern American city, the host pastor called on a theology professor to lead in prayer.

The learned man of God stood before the microphone and I quote him verbatim: *'Lord, you created the heavens and the earth. You created man and you didn't do it by some evolutionary process....'*

Well, well, well, that bit of news must have been an eye-opener for God!

• Another true story is told by a distinguished conference speaker of a tragic plane crash which resulted in the death of all persons aboard. During the morning session, the conference director called on a man to pray. The gentleman in question felt a burden on his heart to pray for the bereaved families.

Unable to recall the location of the disaster, he said: *'Lord, bless that plane crash out there in – out there in – out there in – well, Lord, you know where it is, you must have heard it on CNN this morning!'*

When we hear a prayer like that, we cannot help but wonder, is it sense or nonsense?

Prayer is ...

In the final analysis, prayer is not a shopping list, it is not a rushing in and out of the presence of God with a long list of requests. Prayer is taking quality time to linger and wait in the Lord's presence, adoring and worshipping him.

The prayer that wins God's approval is the one which is prayed *'in the Holy Spirit'*. This means we must really begin to appreciate some of the wonder and aura surrounding his name. He is the Holy Spirit. He is someone with a real and distinctive, living personality.

The Greek word translated, *pneuma*, intimates that the Holy Spirit and the Holy Ghost are interchangeable terms. At the same time, he is someone who is divine for he is God the Holy Spirit. An integral part of the Holy Spirit's work is to make us aware of the gap between the way things should be and the way things are, as understood from the Bible.

It's me, it's me, it's me, O Lord ...

Before we pray we seek to understand his unique ministry in our hearts and lives. It is only when we see who he is and what he is that we will be inclined to give him his rightful place. The fact that we do engage our hearts in prayer seems to suggest that we have a definite need in our lives. Otherwise, why bother?

It means we need God to step into the prevailing situation and intervene. It is a frank and honest admission of our total helplessness. It is a feeling of inadequacy. It is a recognition of our dependence upon him and that he alone is able to meet the deep need in our hearts.

When we pray, we have concluded that he alone can provide the answers to our problems and he is the only one who can undo the tangles we find ourselves in. The simple fact is, we are no match for the powers of darkness in our own strength, we are no match for the enemy no matter how clever we think we are theologically.

The Nike philosophy ... just do it!

We may not feel like praying but that is always the time to do it. We may not feel up to it, we may be unprepared, we may be caught on the back foot, we may be spiritually below par. Prayer is not always easy but we must give ourselves to it. The longer we delay, the more we put it on the back burner, the more used we will become to living our lives without him. We will eventually become conditioned to such a cool relationship that we will spiritually begin to shiver and ultimately our salvation will become a frozen asset.

Praying in the Spirit brings both clarity and courage to our hearts and minds. The fact is, we are never so strong as when we are in prayer.

Kneeling knees do not knock!

Waiting for your call

God is waiting on the end of the line for us to call him. The way is opened up because of his finished work at Calvary and the thrilling truth is that the lines are open now. We have instant and constant access to the Father. His number is never engaged!

The hotline to heaven is never too busy!

We are surrounded by him daily and know his presence and power but we should be surrendered to him. It is a matter of my will being one with his and my all being placed on the altar for God. This is praying in the will of God, this is the prayer that never fails or falters. This is the one prayer that God always answers in the affirmative.

This is probably the one critical factor in all our deliberations before the throne of grace. It is a magic moment when we sense that there is a blending of minds and a fusing together of purpose, when the desires of our heart are in sync with his. When that happens there is an affinity with the infinite Spirit of God.

Staying in touch

I think one of the most important things to grasp about prayer is also one of the simplest, namely, prayer is possible. If 'prayer is the Christian's vital breath', how many believers there are who are gasping, puffing, panting, and short of breath. The painful question is, is that not a slow way to die? When the lines of communication are closed, slowly but surely it leads to a breakdown in that relationship.

That is equally true when we face up to the perennial problem of a lack of prayer. When we fail to intercede, we are the losers. When that happens, we find ourselves on a path that leads to spiritual bankruptcy. We are going off the rails for we are on a line that ends with spiritual asphyxiation. The truth is, we cannot point the finger at someone else, we only have ourselves to blame if we are labelled suffocated saints!

It appears that many of us prefer to inhale the polluted atmosphere of this world and, in the process, do untold damage to our souls, rather than breathe in the fresh air of heaven which guarantees spiritual health.

Jude invites us to get up out of our seats and get down to where the action is. He wants us to be involved on the field of play! He challenges us with a couple of rousing 'get a move on' kind of comments …

- be a player, and
- be a prayer!

11

The fresh air of survival

'Keep yourselves in God's love as you wait for the mercy of our Lord Jesus Christ to bring you to eternal life.'

verse 21

The third factor in Jude's four pronged manifesto is to *'keep yourselves in God's love'*.

- If *'building'* involves a labouring in the Scriptures, and
- *'praying'* implies a leaning on the Spirit, then
- *'keeping'* infers we should be living in the sunshine.

Many years ago Henry Drummond wrote a best selling classic based on an exposition of 1 Corinthians 13 which he called, *The Greatest Thing in the World*.

Love is the greatest thing in all the world!

This particular theme has also captured the imagination of many of our poets whose lines have brought cheer and consolation to millions whose hearts are aching and whose minds are filled with anxiety. A vast number of our favourite hymns have this concept as their dominant message. Stanza after stanza sees the unfolding of this majestic note that finds its fullest manifestation at Calvary.

This chord is ever strung on the harps of the redeemed band in heaven. These lyrics are like a lingering fragrance in the mind of the saint. They mean so much that words cannot adequately convey their intrinsic worth.

Outside looking in

Having said that, the love of God is one of the most seriously misunderstood subjects in the wide field of religion. Men (many of whom have more than a passing interest in theology) who deny the plenary inspiration of Scripture speak freely about the love of God, yet there is no accurate verbal description of God's love apart from that which appears in the Bible.

If the Bible is not the word of God, how do we know that God is love?

We cannot find this great fact in nature. It is not an integral part of modern man's intuitive knowledge. Missionaries returning from all parts of the pagan world tell us that the heathen know nothing of a loving God, never mind a God of love. They have their gods, angry gods, constantly demanding appeasement.

A view from the top

Christianity is unique in that it is the only religion that claims a supreme Being of love. When we stop and think about the love of God, the scene is unrivalled in its breathtaking splendour. From the brow of the highest hill, where our vision is unblurred and unbroken, the towering peaks of the attributes of God lie before us in all their unparalleled glory. There, to the fore, in yonder range of hills, is a summit that has never been conquered by man. It is appropriately designated *'the love of God'*.

I want us to take up our stance and peer through our looking glass from different angles in order to bring this prominent peak into sharp focus. In so doing, we will secure a saint's eye view of this elevated projection. There are certain predominant features which, when pieced together, provide a panoramic picture of his love.

Such love, springs from eternity

We recognise and gratefully acknowledge that his love is a sovereign love. This is the love of God and, as such, it is a love that is exercised by someone who is in full and absolute control of all that is happening around us. He is the Ruler of the universe and his kingdom is one where every decision is seen to be the outworking of his great love for us. Never will he deny himself! He cannot!

This is the love of a crowned monarch who is seated upon a throne in the ivory palaces of heaven. It is the virtue of one before whom the angels bow and before whom the hosts of heaven veil their faces.

This aspect of his character is one that influences all that he says as well as being the overriding factor in all that he does. We often hear people talking about the 'dictates of his love' and this is what they mean when they use that long established cliché.

Love is behind every disclosure of his person and love is before every dispensation of his providence.

O perfect love

I am not exaggerating when I say that the love of God is extra-special. The hymn writer had similar thoughts in mind when he penned the words: 'there is no love like the love of Jesus.' Nothing can be compared to the love of God. He is the incomparable Christ and his love is equal to that in its quality. It stands alone as an example *par excellence*.

There is something about his love that marks it out as different. It has the hallmark of deity stamped upon it. It is a perfect love. There is no flaw in his pedigree, there is no fault in his character. This gives sufficient credence to the idea that there is nothing wrong whatsoever with his love.

I love you because ...

We, as the people of God, should have no twinges of misgiving about the way that he loves. The Lord has his own way of doing things and we are a privileged people to be the objects of such love. His limitless love surpasses all our human efforts, it bypasses all our feeble endeavours, and it transcends all our fondest dreams.

In all the Lord's dealings with us, love is the driving force. This is what gives the real impetus to everything he does.

As God, he is motivated by love and by nothing else.

This is a special kind of love!

- It is *out of this world* because it is heavenly, and
- it is *out of the ordinary* because it is divine.

He does what he does because he is who he is

There is a spontaneity to the love of God. This would suggest that when his love is released for the benefit of others that it is a voluntary act on his part. Never at any time is there a need for coercion. Pressure is never applied and force is never necessary just to get him to love.

Because he is always positive in his outlook towards his people, he never needs to be talked or cajoled into loving us. When he loves, he does it because he wants to do it. When his love touches your heart and mine, it is because he wishes to do it.

Even when we do not respond the way that we should, it makes no difference for he keeps on loving because of who he actually is.

I can't stop loving you

We live in a world where the fortunes of men fluctuate almost on a daily basis. In a vacillating environment, the good news is, the love of God is a constant love. It is unaffected by change.

The love of God is a steadfast love. This is a sublime truth firmly embedded in the Old Testament where we have the oft-repeated word 'lovingkindness'.

It may be a term as old as the hills but it has its roots in the eternal character of God. It is one that conveys the idea of *chesed*, the Hebrew expression for 'steadfast love'.

When, at times, our love ebbs and flows, his is a love that remains the same. It never reaches an all-time high and it never plummets to an all-time low. Thank God, his love is not like the proverbial yo-yo. It is changeless!

The day God died

There is so much more we could say about the love of God, let me give you a couple of thoughts and you can meditate on them at your leisure. The love of God is a supernatural love. We find that echoed in the prayer of the apostle Paul in Ephesians 3:14-21 where he was overwhelmed with the sheer vastness of the love of God. It is like a reservoir that never runs dry!

The love of God is unmeasured, and immeasurable.

When we put the spotlight on the cross at Calvary we quickly recognise that this love is a sacrificial love. This is love in its greatest and highest expression. It is very difficult to evaluate a love such as his. At the same time, we cannot fail to be impressed with the incredible wonder of it all. There is an air of mystery attached to it.

24:7

And yet, when all is said and done, this is no pie-in-the-sky philosophy. There is nothing airy-fairy about it. It has down-to-earth implications associated with it for it impacts every area of our lives.

The life and love of Christ are set before us in the word of God as an example to follow. Here is someone we must attempt to emulate, all day, every day. When we make love our aim, then we are actively walking in the footsteps of Jesus. In that unique sense, his love is a standard. Paul develops that particular theme in 1 Corinthians 13:1 where he calls it 'the most excellent way'.

That is why when we *'keep ourselves in the love of God'* we are living in the sunshine!

The litmus test

Jude is no ignoramus. Let us make no mistake about it, he has his head well screwed on. This is abundantly clear from the comments he has made earlier in his epistle. We can be absolutely certain he knows exactly what he is talking about.

He has proven in his own experience that this is something that works and that is always the acid test. With penetrating insight, he is all too familiar with the problems we face and here he describes the remedy. This is the cure for all our ills, this is the solution to all our mounting crises.

We all agree with the proposition made and we are unanimous in our approval of such an intelligent idea. Having said that, how many of us know anything about it in our personal lives? That is when the crunch comes. Why is that the case? Because Jude has placed the ball fairly and squarely into our court. If you like, the onus is on us.

A hands on approach

It is solely our responsibility to keep ourselves. The Greek word *tēreō* is one of Jude's favourite words. He uses it a number of times to develop his theme in the epistle.

The punchline is, we have to keep ourselves, no-one else can do it for us.

We cannot share it and we cannot shelve it. We cannot duck our responsibility. We are accountable to God for our stewardship of this weighty challenge. This is an exercise we need to constantly work at. It is something we need to work out for ourselves. There is no proviso made for abdicating saints. If we fall at this fence, our progress in spiritual matters will be greatly impeded and our vision of attaining spiritual maturity will be grossly impaired.

If we falter here, we have reached our Waterloo!

It is a daunting task to say the least and, at face value, it may appear to be a tough assignment. We will need to mobilise all our resources within if we are to stay in such a wonderful position of being in the love of God.

Two sides of one coin

I think it is helpful for us to realise that this term is a paradox. On the face of it, it seems to be a contradiction of what is mentioned in verse 1 when Jude says we are *'kept by Jesus Christ'*. This is the divine side of the coin which is stamped with the words, eternal security. In verse 21, however, we have the human side of the same coin. We keep ourselves as though the entire enterprise were up to us, knowing, at the same time, that God keeps us as though our fidelity were irrelevant. This, therefore, makes it complementary.

Actually, these two aspects of the one doctrine are like parallel lines. They never meet, but an over-emphasis on either creates an imbalance which results in one going off at a tangent. Herein lies the great danger.

Many believers have made shipwreck of their lives by laying too much emphasis on the sovereign ability of God and, at the same time, failing to realise fully the responsibility of human beings in his family.

On the other hand, quite a number are spiritual castaways today because they majored on man's part to the neglect of God's part in this unique situation. Having said that, we must be extremely careful to steer a middle course thereby averting an accident with needless casualties. The risk of going off the track is greatly reduced when we exercise spiritual caution.

Spiritual resolution

This, surely, is an awesome task. It may appear a tough assignment, and it is! The fact is, with God's help we can do it! If we are to achieve our goal of spiritual success then it is essential that we maximise our energies so that we may attain this coveted position of being *'in the love of God'*.

That will mean considerable resolve on our part. It will involve strength of character to withstand the attacks of the enemy. It will mean a spirit of dogged determination being manifested in our actions. It will entail a mobilising of all our resources in Christ so that we stand immovable in that sphere. Steadfastness is vital if our position is to be consolidated. All the grace he has placed at our disposal will be required by us if we are to realise our ambition and be found in the place of his appointment.

Location, location, location

When God calls, God equips!

Those words are amazingly appropriate in this connection. God is calling us to a definite location for he wants us to be *'in the love of God'*.

Because this is his will for your life and mine, it means it is for our good. His way is always the best way. Obviously, a great lack prevails in our lives and the only way we can be where he wishes us to be is for him to supply our need, however large or small. When we avail ourselves of his gracious provision, then and only then, are we able to move forward.

When we think about this incredible phrase there is a lot more to it than meets the eye. There always is! Think about the vantage of such a location. What a wonderful place to be in. How glorious the setting. How delightful the location. When we arrive at this splendid destination, the very atmosphere is different. The surroundings pay silent testimony to the handiwork of the great Creator who became our Saviour.

Length of stay?

It is one thing to arrive at such a place with an overnight bag, it is quite a different matter putting down our roots and staying in such a place. It is possible ...

* to be a frequent visitor and come and go as one pleases,
* to be a day tripper or even take a one night stand,
* to enjoy a weekend sunshine break and earn a few days respite from the occupational hazards of life.

On the other hand, the one who derives the greatest possible benefit from staying at such a location is not the casual visitor or the bed and breakfast lodger, but the person who prolongs his stay and sets up home in the sunshine.

The grass is greener on the other side

Perhaps the best illustration of this concept is found in the parable of the prodigal son in Luke 15:11-32. Here was a young man who turned his back on home and all that it stood for. He had had enough! For him, faraway fields were green. The fact is, how quickly they changed colour! He soon remembered that home was evergreen, when he felt homesick. A few month's earlier, he had been sick of home!

As a young lad, he lost virtually everything.

* Sin robbed him of his capital and it stripped him of his character. Now the poor fella is destitute and living like a tramp.
* He lost his silver, he has no money, he does not have two pennies to rub together. The jingle has gone from his pockets leaving only a gaping

hole.

- He lost his sanctity when he indulged heavily in riotous living. For him, life is just one big horrible mess.
- He lost his self-respect as he laboured among the pigs, he was doing something which was culturally unacceptable. How he trails his feet along the gutter of depravity.
- He lost his smile because he is a picture of despair and his cry is one of desperation, 'I perish with hunger'. He has a forlorn look on his face. If the truth be told, the joy has gone out of his life.

Where is my wandering boy tonight?

All of the time the boy was away from home, the father never changed in his attitude towards him. He was still his son and he really loved him. However, the problem is this, the son had removed himself from the place where he could enjoy to the full the benefits of his father's love.

He was not in the place where his father could bless him. He was the loser. He gained absolutely nothing from flirting with the world. He had nothing to show for his mad spending spree when he painted the town red.

He could look back in later years and put it all down to experience, albeit a bad one. He could sport the tee-shirt and testify, been there, done that!

He knows in his heart of hearts that he is the one who really missed out.

Home, sweet, home

Now that he is back home, he appreciates his father's love more than he did before. You see, to be in the sphere and environment of the Father's love is to be what he wants us to be and to be where he wants us to be. And that is what Jude encourages us to do.

When we return to him after living in the barren land of sin and shame, he gladly welcomes us back to where we belong. And when we are there, we enjoy again the warmth of the rays of his love as they beam toward us. It is there that we bask contentedly underneath the sunshine of his tender compassion.

What a change that is for us when we compare it with our days in self-imposed exile. Surely this is the most logical place for any of us to set up our spiritual home. We could dwell in no better area than this. In that sense, location is what really counts!

In the future tense

'Christianity makes sense only if the promises God makes are kept.'

That statement is particularly relevant in the light of Jude's closing comment in verse 21 of his stirring epistle. It is item number four in his spiritual manifesto for the people of God. He says, I want you to *'wait for the mercy of our Lord Jesus Christ to bring you to eternal life'*. This is a forward look. It is all about living our lives in the future tense.

So far as we are concerned, God's promises are still waiting for their final fulfilment and until then we pin our destiny on the future rather than the present.

We live today in the light of tomorrow, we live today in the light of eternity. It is the coming of Christ that makes the significant difference.

This is why Jude's last point of his four-point plan is so vitally important. His simple and clearly defined strategy which will lead to spiritual success is dependent on our following closely each suggestion he makes. We are ...

* *labouring in the Scriptures,*
* *leaning on the Spirit,*
* *living in the sunshine, and*
* *looking for the Saviour.*

Each of these four ideas can be neatly summarised in one word which will help us retain them in our hearts for future spiritual benefit and blessing. For example,

* in *'building'* there is edification,
* in *'praying'* there is supplication,

- in *'keeping'* there is preservation, and
- in *'waiting'* there is expectation.

A days march nearer home

It becomes increasingly apparent as we ponder over this phrase that there are two key words, *'wait'* and *'mercy'*. One speaks of an act and the other speaks of an attribute. If the first is indicative of the response in a believer's heart to the news of Jesus' soon return, then the second is a reflection of a quality found inherent in the character of Christ.

Because of who he is, and what he is, we ought to be living in anticipation of his advent at any moment. We should be living each day as if it were our last day. The fact is, today we are one day nearer home than we were at this time yesterday.

Saved by good looks

I am sure many of you are familiar with the lyrics of the song, 'there is life for a look at the ....' As we gaze upon Jesus, we view him in various capacities as he ministers on our behalf. My enjoyment of the life he imparts is determined by my appreciation of the service he renders for me in the glory. The life he offers us is varied and is best understood when we realise that the 'look' and the 'life' are linked together.

When we turn our eyes upon Jesus we discover there is everlasting life for a look at the crucified one! What a place to start. We could find no better! As we collect our many thoughts that centre around the cross, our hearts will be drawn out after him. This is holy ground we are standing on. We must tread carefully and cautiously lest we fall into the trap of exalting man and not extolling the glories of God's grace.

Musings on mercy

Here we breathe the air of heaven. Here we hear the heartbeat of the Father. When we stop for a brief moment and think of our Saviour, we realise the Bible is packed full with verses pertaining to this aspect of his impeccable character.

Woven throughout the Scriptures is the thread of the mercy of God. From Genesis to Revelation this is the grandest theme. When we observe the dealings of God with men in days gone past it is clear that his mercy played a key role. It was often directed towards the individual and was also seen in his handling of national crises.

Mercy is the symbol of the government of God in the affairs of men.

Throughout we are given the tremendous privilege of considering the beneficence of a loving heavenly Father. Moses speaks of the greatness of the mercy of God and how Israel as a redeemed people proved those words day after day (*cf.* Numbers 14:18). When they murmured and moaned and deserved the worst, in return, they had mercy extended towards them.

Yet, mercy has its limits! After 'tempting God these ten times' they were prevented from entering into the land of promise (*cf.* Jude 5).

Not a seven day wonder

One note is recorded many times in the Old Testament and it is that his mercy endures forever. It is not something transient or fleeting, it is not here today and gone tomorrow. The mercy of God is not a flash in a pan. It is here to stay. It is from everlasting to everlasting, it is beyond our wildest dreams, it is outside the confines of time. His mercy is ageless and eternal (*cf.* 2 Chronicles 7:3).

When contemplating the need in his own heart in Psalm 86, David is suddenly overwhelmed with the realisation that God is abounding in mercy. Surely this is a reminder to all of us that there is no limit to his resources. They are never in short supply.

No matter how great or intense the need may be, the brook of God's mercy never runs dry.

From the Old, to the New

The Psalms and prophets combine to pay eloquent tribute to the mercy of God, it is a fitting testimony to the unfailing kindness of God. Much is made of the mercy of God in the New Testament as well. For example, Zechariah gratefully acknowledges that remission of sin is only achieved through the tender mercy of God (*cf.* Luke 1:78). This suggests that his mercy comes from the innermost part of his being. It emanates from a heart of love and compassion. There is emotion in the mercy of God. There is a depth of feeling found there that is difficult to explain.

Peter and Paul walked down similar paths when they extolled the wonderful mercy of God in their own lives and they are both thrilled when they see it in the lives of others. It reaches you, it reaches me. It is as personal as that! We are debtors to mercy alone!

The mercy seat

The question is: how did it all come about? Through the cross of our Lord Jesus Christ! That is why we need to see him, first and foremost, as the crucified one. It was on that dark hillside of Calvary that mercy and truth met together. What a great meeting that must have been.

It is there that Christ became the propitiation or mercy seat for our sins (*cf.* 1 John 2:2). The use of the word 'propitiation' (Greek, *hilasmos*) brings out clearly that mercy has no saving merit apart from the death of Jesus. It can also be translated 'mercy seat' and that is worth explaining.

The mercy seat was the lid or covering on the ark of the covenant. It was ordered of God and it became the place where God met and communed with Moses. It was on the mercy seat that the high priest put the blood once a year on the Day of Atonement, the feast of Yom Kippur.

It is always associated with the covering or removal of sin. So, when Christ is said to be the propitiation for our sins, it means that through his blood God extends the mercy of his justifying grace to the believing sinner.

The blood on the mercy seat of the ark was a type of the blood of Christ shed for sinners. Thus the one who shed his blood becomes the mercy seat where God meets the sinner and extends his mercy to him.

Thank God, there is mercy with the Lord!

Fair exchange

There is an exchanged life for a look at the crowned one! It costs us nothing to become a Christian. Why? Because Jesus paid it all. But it costs everything to be a Christian. That may seem a strange statement to make in this context. Well, not really. Someone has said, 'if he is not Lord of all, then he is not Lord at all!'

There is only one way that can happen. It comes through denying oneself and taking up the cross and following only after him. It means dying daily to self and sin. It means a yielded heart and a living unto God. That thought was uppermost in Paul's mind when he wrote, 'I no longer live, but Christ lives in me' (Galatians 2:20). An exchanged life.

That experience becomes intensely personal in our lives through the *'mercy of our Lord Jesus Christ'*. In other words, if it were not for him, we would not be able to do it. Because of his coronation, the least that I can do is submit myself to him and be a loyal and obedient servant. In every situation, Jesus is Lord and King!

Exciting days ahead!

Life may be upbeat now, but there is better on before! For the Christian, the best is yet to be.

The future is bright for the people of God.

We are bound for the land where roses never fade. We are en route to Immanuel's land. We are born for glory, we are bound for glory, and one day we will be in the glory. Our ultimate destination is the city of God.

The hallmark of our experience is that, to a man, we all know where we are going. Heaven is on the horizon, but one day we will be there. And we will be there before we realise it. Faster than the batting of an eyelid, in the twinkling of an eye, we shall be changed into his likeness. All will be made anew and for evermore we shall be in the presence of him who loved us and gave himself for us.

What a day that will be

Eternity will become a glorious reality. Heaven will be our home. The saints of all the ages will be there sharing the joy of unbroken fellowship with each other and, above all, the bliss of non-stop communion with Jesus. A vast multitude will form God's choir in the sky and sing unto him, 'worthy is the Lamb that was slain'. As they break forth into praise, the angels will listen with wonder and amazement for they have 'never felt the joys that our salvation brings'.

The only reason why any of us will be part and parcel of that illustrious company gathered unto him is down to the *'mercy of our Lord Jesus Christ'*.

• It is mercy that has saved us and brought us to himself.

- It is mercy that has kept us for himself day by day.
- It is mercy that will take us to himself when the sound of the trumpet is heard.

Then his mercy will be complete in our lives when he has us where he wants us to be as a bride by his side. The very thought of such a prospect thrills my soul! It makes me feel very restless and unsettled. It really excites me. It enthrals me.

It leaves me longing for heaven and home.

All's well that ends well

I am reminded of the words found in the Song of Solomon when the bride heard the voice of her beloved and she cried out, 'Look! Here he comes.' (2:8) When he came, he spoke and he said to her with tenderness and affection, 'Arise, my darling, my beautiful one, and come with me.'

Those thoughts are but a shadow of things to come as they draw our attention to the advent of our Saviour, the Lord Jesus Christ. Very soon we shall hear his voice and he will beckon to each one of us, 'arise and come with me'. I can tell you, 'that will be glory for me!'

Like the bride in the love story, we should be looking for him and listening for his voice. We ought to be living not only with expectancy in our hearts but also with a keen sense of anticipation as well. We should be waiting for him to return. And, most certainly, we should be watching for his appearing.

When he comes, mercy will be manifest in that he will bring us *'to eternal life'*. This is something we enjoy in our hearts today but in heaven it is something we shall fully experience. The very life of God is our present portion, but the quality of such a life will be enhanced considerably when we leave this world behind us.

The richness of such an existence is beyond belief. Nevertheless, it will be our lot and, again, because of his mercy, 'our lines have fallen in pleasant places'. Eternity will not only mean the life of God in our souls but the inheritance reserved for us involves life with God for an unending period.

This is the grand finale and that is why Jude implores us to be *'waiting for the Saviour'*. He knows it is for our good, but more than that, it will redound to his honour and glory.

In that day and on that resurrection morning when the shadows flee away, his marvellous mercy will be magnified in his Son and in those whom he has washed in his blood.

Approaching zero hour

The second advent of Jesus is imminent and impending. When we read the signs of the times – and apostasy is one of them – we become increasingly convinced that we cannot be around here too much longer. Because of that, we will want to be ready to meet the Lord as he breaks through the clouds.

Anticipating the sound of the trumpet, we will be sitting on the edge of our seats, we will be standing on our tiptoes. The countdown is getting lower every day. It will soon be zero hour. Then we will be with him. That will be the icing on the cake for the real believer.

The synthetic saints will be left behind to face the judgment of God. Their prospects, as we have seen already, are doom and gloom. The future of the Christian, however, is bright and beaming.

It is something to get really excited about. We should be jumping for joy.

This terrific news is designed to put the sparkle back into drab and dreary lives.

Success is guaranteed

I think Jude has given us a lot of food for serious thought. He has given us a programme with four main suggestions. If we pursue his plan of action faithfully, success will be ours in time and in eternity. Now we shine as lights in a dark world of sin. Then we shall shine as the stars of the morning.

- 'Building' entails a working with our minds,
- 'praying' involves a waiting upon our knees,
- 'keeping' denotes a warming of our hearts, and
- 'waiting' implies a watching with our eyes!

Only God can help us, but when we stop and think about it, that is what he is there for. And, so far as his mercy is concerned, well, that is available also.

A well-rounded individual

The picture we have here is of a thorough Christian. You see, a Christian is one who builds, prays, keeps, and waits. A Christian builds his life on the gospel which is the word of God. A Christian prays with the aid of the Holy Spirit. Christians treasure the love God has for them and keep the flame of love for God burning in their hearts and lives. Christians are those who look beyond this present life and wait with great expectancy and joy for the coming of the Lord. This is what we need to be up and doing as Christians, no matter what our circumstances.

Recently I came across a story which touched my heart and it serves to illustrate what Jude is saying here. It is the true story of a Chinese pastor who spent eighteen years in prison for his faith.

In 1991 he gave this remarkable testimony: *'The authorities put me to work emptying the human waste cesspool. But they didn't know in those years how much I enjoyed working there. It was 2 metres square and filled with human waste ... I had to walk into the disease-ridden mass and scoop out successive layers ... so why did I enjoy working in the cesspool? In the labour camp, all the prisoners were normally kept under fairly strict surveillance, but all the guards and prisoners kept their distance from the cesspool because of the putrid smell.*

'When I worked there, I could be alone and I could pray to the Lord as loudly as I needed. I could recite the Scriptures, including all the Psalms I still remembered, and no-one was close enough to protest. I could raise my voice and sing all the hymns I still remembered ... again and again as I praised the Lord in the cesspool, I experienced the closeness of the Lord's presence ... in that sense, the cesspool became my private garden where I met the Lord.'

That is amazing, isn't it! Through his praying in the Spirit, and building himself up in the Scriptures, and his rejoicing in the love of God, the prison cesspool became a veritable garden of Eden. That proves it works in the rough and tumble of everyday life!

Healthy living

What we have here is a New Testament recipe for a healthy spiritual life even during times of trial and trouble in the churches and in the world. Jude says, do not sit back and do not be passive! Stand up and take responsibility for yourselves! Four words say it all: build, pray, keep, and wait!

As we take a quiet moment and look back on our lives, I am sure many of us can identify with David when he says, 'surely goodness and mercy have followed me all the days of my life'. As we contemplate the future, we do so with a high level of confidence for we know 'we shall dwell in the Lord's house forever'.

Charles Wesley was on the same wavelength when he penned those few words of lasting meaning:

> *'Tis mercy all, immense and free,*
> *for, O, my God, it found out me!*

12

Rescue the perishing

'Be merciful to those who doubt; snatch others from the fire and save them; to others show mercy, mixed with fear – hating even the clothing stained by corrupted flesh.'

verses 22, 23

Taking responsibility seriously

The story of General Charles George Gordon (1833-85) sets a simple but consummate example. He was the nineteenth century British soldier who won lasting fame, eventually losing his life in the defence of Khartoum.

He served his country well but declined both a title and a financial reward offered to him by the British government. After some persuasion he accepted a gold medal inscribed with a record of his thirty-three military engagements and this medal became his most prized possession.

After his death, however, it could not be found. It was only later, when his diaries were found, that it was discovered that, on hearing news of a severe famine, he had sent the gold medal to be melted down and used to buy bread for the poor. He had written in his diary, *'The last earthly thing I had in this world that I valued I have given to the Lord Jesus Christ today.'*

As a Christian man, General Gordon wanted to do his best to take responsibility for others, following the example of his Saviour.

Others!

In this duo of verses we are introduced to three groups of people who need our attention. We are encouraged to reach out to these needy souls with the message that Jesus is mighty and strong to save. Jude explains how a strong and secure Christian can help the feeble, fragile, frail, and weak-kneed.

It is wonderful to note that the last admonition of Jude, like the last words of the Lord Jesus whom he served, have to do with soul winning. Here is evangelism at its best and most effective.

We either evangelise or fossilise!

Each one, reach one

So far as Jude is concerned, that is the bottom line. The burden is resting squarely on our shoulders to win the lost to Jesus. This is the least we can do for the Lord especially when we think of how much he has done for us.

When our eyes have caught the vision that Jesus is soon returning and our hearts have felt the thrill of all that implies, then we really have no other option but to reach out to others. This is the sacred duty of every believer toward those who have not yet been born again.

In fact, this should not surprise us, because our God is a God who oozes compassion. No matter how terrible his judgments may be, or how dreadful the doom he has decreed for those who deny the Lord Jesus, God dearly and deeply loves those who are enticed by the men of whom this epistle speaks.

To that end, he has commissioned all who know the truth to seek and to save the lost by presenting to them the good news of a full and free salvation. No sooner have we finished reading what we are to do for ourselves in the presence of ungodly mockers than we discover that these truths do not stand alone. They are inseparable from the truth of what we are to do for those around us. There is certainly no interruption in the flow of thought between verses 21 and 23. We cannot escape these instructions concerning personal witness.

- Every Christian is an evangelist.
- Every believer is a missionary.
- Each individual sinner we meet is a prospective mission field and someone needing evangelism.

Pigeon-holing people

John Benton asks the question: *'Why has Christ left the church on earth when most things we do in the church could be done better in heaven?'*

It is simply because we are left here as witnesses! These verses make very clear our solemn responsibility to those travelling the road to hell. With the love of God in our hearts, we are able to show mercy to sinful men so that, ultimately, they may know the joy of sins forgiven. You see, compassion is the name of the game. Right belief is useless if it lacks compassion. Someone has said, 'People do not care how much we know until they know how much we care!'

Jude sets out three missions to rescue fallen people. The question is, what is the identity of these people to whom Jude is referring? They are:

- those who need compassionate tenderness because sincere doubts trouble them,
- those requiring urgent boldness if they are to be snatched from an eternity of fiery judgment, and
- those who must be dealt with cautiously lest the soul winner himself be contaminated by their sins.

How important it is for us to understand the peculiar needs of each group so that we might see the gospel triumph in their hearts.

Changed lives are what we are looking for.

That is only possible through the gospel of the grace of God for it alone is the power of God unto salvation. I want us to look at each one of these groups separately and seek to understand more fully what it means to rescue the perishing.

Doubters!

The first group are those in doubt! We, as the Lord's own people, are the recipients of great mercy. It is multiplied to us now (*cf.* verse 2) and we look with eager anticipation for an abundant manifestation of it in the future at the return of our Saviour in power and glory (*cf.* verse 21). It is only fitting, therefore, that we should be merciful to others.

We are surrounded in today's world by people who are enmeshed in a net of doubt, people who do not really know what is right or true. They are not necessarily antagonistic toward Christianity, they are just not sure about it. And, because of that, they are in turmoil.

We often say that such folk are 'really open to the truth', but they are also usually open to untruth. As John MacArthur points out, 'While listening to the gospel of Jesus Christ, they may also be listening to Jehovah's Witnesses or to Mormons.'

People need to ask honest questions. But we should be there with a listening ear and an understanding heart when they do. Unless we obey what Jude is saying to us their upfront doubts will give way to eternal despair. That would be, to say the least, an appalling and unnecessary tragedy.

First and last

It is wonderfully instructive to look back at the first use of this word *'mercy'* (Greek, *eleeō*) in the New Testament. It is enshrined in the promise we read in Matthew 5:7 where it says: 'Blessed are the merciful, for they will be shown mercy.' It is profitable to place this passage alongside the last use of this word in the Bible which is the portion now before us.

Who are the 'merciful' of whom Christ spoke? Certainly they would include those who have compassion on the lost and seek to win them to the Saviour. When do they obtain mercy? Although multiplied to them throughout life, it is received in greatest measure when all the fulness of eternal life dawns upon the soul at the second coming of Jesus for his church. Blessed indeed are all soul winners! 'Blessed' means 'happy' and no greater joy is to be found than the joy of extending mercy to the lost by bringing them to a personal experience of salvation.

It is interesting to note that the gospel of Matthew also presents the first use of the word *'doubt'* (*cf.* Matthew 14:31). He used the Greek word *distazō* implying 'uncertainty which way to take'. In hermeneutics (the science of interpreting the Bible), the Law of First Mention states that the first occurrence of a word in the Scriptures often underlines something significant about its later usage.

Keeping your head above water

Matthew records the familiar story of how Peter heard the invitation of Christ to come to him on the waters. Peter, bless him, started out well but fear soon filled his heart and he began to sink into the blue waters of the Sea of Galilee. When Peter cried out in a moment of panicked desperation, 'Lord, save me!' we read that 'immediately Jesus reached out his hand and caught him.' When Jesus grabbed Peter by the hand, he said to him, 'You of little faith, why did you doubt?'

We need to keep this record to the front of our minds as we study Jude's epistle. Despite the Saviour's open invitation to come, many folk remain fearful and apprehensive. Because they doubt his ability and power to save, they are ready to sink into the oblivion of perdition.

Such folk are slowly sinking in the quicksand of time and, at the end of the day, they will be hopelessly lost in the great sea of eternity.

As his representatives on planet earth, we are to reach out the hand of compassion and tell them all they need is a cry of helpless trust, 'Lord, save me!'

Option B

Another rendering of this verse is given in the margin, 'and some refute while they dispute with you'. If this is to be accepted as a better translation of an admittedly difficult Greek text, it is well illustrated for us in verse 9. Michael contended with the devil when he disputed over the body of Moses.

A dispute is sometimes forced upon the soul winner. Although it is true that getting into an argument is usually unwise when dealing with those outside the family of God, here is a passage requiring us to refute or convict those who dispute with us.

To contend and lose is a serious matter, to contend and win is to gain a soul for eternity.

And that is worth everything. That is why we are to be ready to give an answer for the hope that is within us (*cf.* 1 Peter 3:15). We should be prepared to demonstrate the falsity of an opponent's position in the power and wisdom of the Holy Spirit. Our own lack of wisdom in such a situation is the condition for securing the wisdom which God supplies (*cf.* James 1:5).

Old-time conviction

The Holy Spirit tells us to refute or convict those who oppose our witness. We can best do this if we build ourselves up on our most holy faith, pray in the Spirit, keep ourselves in the love of God, and live as those who wait for the coming of Jesus. In our hands, the word of God can become the sword of the Spirit to pierce the heart and a hammer to break down the opposition.

The word 'refute' means more than to persuade successfully. It carries a punitive idea as in Hebrews 12:5 where it is translated 'rebuked' (Greek, *elenchō*) with special reference to the chastening hand of our Father God.

The word of God can refute, convict, and convert.

Bless God, it really can!

A working knowledge

Every born again believer ought to have some personal experience of the meaning of this phrase of Scripture. When the Lord returns, there is no doubt about it, he will convict the ungodly of all their godless works (*cf.* verse 15). Before he comes, however, we have the solemn responsibility of convicting men of their sin by his word in the power of the Holy Spirit.

If we succeed, and that should be our prayerful dream and aspiration, they will escape the judgment foretold by Enoch. The choice is theirs – they may choose between being convicted now or being convicted then.

The difference is as great as the width of the chasm dividing heaven and hell.

Now we begin to understand the reason why the task before us is so urgent to reach out to the doubting soul.

Dicing with danger!

The second group of people to whom we are called to minister are those in danger! In dealing with this assortment of misguided individuals we cannot afford to be afraid of upsetting them. This class of unsaved people are to be saved by snatching them out of the fire of a lost eternity. It is logical to assume that Jude is referring here to the eternal fire he mentioned up the chapter in verse 7.

We recall how Lot and his two daughters were plucked as brands from the burning (*cf.* Genesis 19). To me, they are a classic example of the people group to which Jude is referring. Actually, the appropriateness of the illustration is underscored by the irony that prayer in the Holy Spirit is found in each context. Jude enjoins this upon us. Genesis 19:27-29 records that the prime reason for the mercy of the Lord being granted to Lot was the intercession of godly Abraham.

One man's prayers made a world of difference!

Too close for comfort

What these men have done who are so near to hell fire, Jude does not inform us, but the story of Lot suggests that they are living in close contact with fleshly sin. I wonder, is there something about such sin that tends to set a man apart from the conviction of the Holy Spirit in some degree so that his danger of perdition is the greater?

It is impossible to state such a suggestion categorically, but passages like Mark 9:42-48 may imply something like this. Matthew 5:22 states that a man who calls his brother a 'fool' is in danger of Gehenna, while Matthew 23:33 raises the question of how a hypocrite can escape the damnation of hell.

Eternal punishment is real! I believe it because the Bible teaches it. In fact, that is one of the greatest motivational influences for engaging in evangelism. If I did not believe in hell, I do not think I would have any real heart to preach the gospel of Jesus Christ.

William Booth, founder of the Salvation Army, apologised to his first graduating class of officers for having kept them for two years to be taught how to lead a soul to Christ. He said, *'It would be far better if you were to spend five minutes in hell. Then you would need no further training.'*

Light from the past

There are two other Old Testament examples that are directly related to this passage in Jude. Amos the 'country cousin' prophet has referred to Israel as 'a burning stick snatched from the fire' (Amos 4:11). And the royal prophet, Zechariah, describes Joshua the high priest of Israel as standing before the angel of the Lord with Satan standing at his right hand to resist him. He writes: 'the Lord said to Satan, "The Lord, who has chosen Jerusalem, rebuke you! Is not this man a burning stick snatched from the fire?"' (Zechariah 3:1, 2).

It is hard to imagine that even the high priest of Israel was a man who had been snatched from the flames. I think this should encourage us to hope that some of those who now seem hopelessly lost in sin may become useful servants of Christ if we heed the Scriptures and pluck them out. No case should be regarded as hopeless. There is no person who is so irredeemably bad that God's forgiveness cannot remove the stain (*cf.* Isaiah 30:22).

None are beyond the grace of God. People *can* be saved!

The history of soul winning is filled with copious records of men and women so far gone in sin that it seemed as though the flames of hell were about to receive them, that is, until some humble messenger of the cross told them about Jesus and rescued them out of the fire, and they went on to become outstanding evangelists and personal workers. Praise God, he is just the same today!

Surely this is what the blind poet, Fanny Crosby, had in mind when she penned these incisive and perceptive words:

Rescue the perishing, care for the dying,
Snatch them in pity from sin and the grave;
Weep o'er the erring one, lift up the fallen,
Tell them of Jesus, the mighty to save.

Down in the human heart, crushed by the tempter,
Feelings lie buried that grace can restore;
Touched by a loving heart, wakened by kindness,
Chords that were broken will vibrate once more.

Rescue the perishing, duty demands it!
Strength for your labour the Lord will provide;
Back to the narrow way, patiently win them,
Tell the poor wanderer a Saviour has died.

Rescue the perishing, care for the dying;
Jesus is merciful, Jesus will save.

Goners!

The third class of sinners with whom we are told to deal are those who have departed from the faith. Jude exhorts us to approach them with fear. We are not told that they are in a worse condition than those who are to be pulled from the flames, but that we are in greater danger in dealing with them, even though they may not be themselves on the verge of perdition.

Don't rush in where angels fear to tread

We would hardly consider ourselves to be in danger of spiritual contamination when we are dealing with a poor drunkard who is reeling precariously on the edge of eternity or a condemned inmate of a high security prison.

Yet, there are types of sin and groups of sinners which not only threaten the spiritual life of the enthusiastic and zealous soul winner but which have actually ensnared more than one servant of Christ.

Satan will do all in his power to make an instrument in the hand of God end up as a spiritual wreck washed up on the shores of time.

The words of Paul in 1 Corinthians 9:27 are so relevant at this point that 'having preached to others, I myself will not be disqualified for the prize'. God forbid! We dare not adopt the ostrich mentality and bury our head in the sand! The sombre facts have got to be faced realistically, it has happened.

Most Christian leaders know of cases where a once-useful follower of the Lord fell into grievous fleshly sin because he did not heed Jude's warning. Solomon, in all his wisdom, illustrated this very point of mingling our zeal with godly fear when he penned the book of Proverbs.

Fallen heroes

Sadly and regrettably, some folk have thought they could better win their friends and work mates by engaging in social drinking, only to become eventually enslaved by it. Other folk have lost their effectiveness in evangelism through covetousness during a ministry among the well-to-do where money talks.

There is for some folk a very real temptation to try to win those who oppose the truth by toning down the gospel or compromising with unbelief. There is a tendency in some circles to water down the claims of the Lord Jesus. How sad it is when men dilute the gospel story just to appease a listening audience.

Sex appeal

I think, perhaps, the commonest incidence of failure to listen to Jude's admonition is found in ministry to members of the opposite sex. One of the basic and fundamental rules of successful soul winning is that it is wise to deal with one's own sex – man to man, woman to woman.

The person who ignores this precept, who forgets the many faithful warnings of Proverbs, who defiantly overlooks the last principle of witness set forth by Jude, does so at his peril.

Sin has a way of tripping up the best of men.

Dirty clothes

However, Jude does not stop there as he proceeds to exhort us that we should hate *'even the clothing stained by corrupted flesh'*. What on earth is he talking about? Well, in a touch of irony, there is a striking parallel between Jude 22, 23 and Zechariah 3:1-5.

We can safely suggest that Zechariah throws light upon Jude by placing a threefold illustration before the soul winner. Those who dispute with us are actually tools of Satan who must be rebuked in the name of the Lord Jesus if we are going to win them. Again, those whom we pluck from the fire are individuals in whom the Lord has a personal interest, and we may count upon his help in our superhuman task.

- He stands with us,
- his word directs us,
- his Spirit empowers us, and
- his love encompasses even those whose sin is like an evil contagion.

And, finally

All those whom Jude here describes must be seen as God sees them, as clothed in filthy garments. There may be superficial or even a very real attractiveness about some forms of sin, else we would not be warned concerning some types of sinners. But, at the end of the day, sin is sin is sin. And beyond the surface, within the aura of glamour, gaiety, and seductive appearance, lurks the filthy garment of soul destroying sin.

It is true that we should love the sinner but we must detest and deplore his sin.

It is customary simply to regard this difficult passage as a proverbial expression. We are to have mercy while hating everything to do with the sin of the men to whom we bear witness, even down to their 'kiton' or inner robe, which is a symbol of all that touches or surrounds the sinner.

As the garment is spotted by the flesh so that atmosphere in which some live is defiled and capable of defiling the child of God. He must hate that atmosphere as well as the environment together with those alluring garments in which sin is sometimes arrayed.

A fine line

If we exhibit true godly fear in dealing with persons whose sin could contaminate us, we will shun their form of sin as we would run a marathon to avoid the plague. We will not go near it with a disinfected barge pole!

We will be as careful as Israel was commanded to be in the presence of leprosy or other communicable diseases. Yet, we will be as merciful and compassionate as we can be in view of what the Scriptures command and what the Holy Spirit enables us to do. When reaching out to others, it is right that we should not be cocksure of ourselves, we need to rely on the Holy Spirit for mental alertness, spiritual perception, and emotional stability.

Jude's four commands leave us in no doubt as to the way to tackle each situation as it presents itself to us. We are:

* to show *mercy* (verse 22),
* to show *urgency* (verse 23a),

- to show *sensitivity* (verse 23b), and
- to show *purity* (verse 23c).

It seems to me that this sound advice should spur us on in our attempts at soul winning. At the same time, we should never let our compassion and courage overshadow our caution! Alan Redpath used to say, 'If it is possible for your closest contacts to be neutral about Christ, then there is something wrong with your Christianity.'

When it comes to talking about Christ, are you a conversational dropout? Could I suggest that someone, somewhere is waiting for you to speak to them about Jesus and his love?

Thank God, someone took the time to share their faith with us and tell us about the Lord Jesus. We want to be numbered among the wise men of this generation, in line with the words of Solomon, for 'he who wins souls is wise' (Proverbs 11:30). John Wesley said to his students, 'You have only one business and that is the salvation of souls.'

Maybe we need to pray with Amy Carmichael:

Oh, for a passionate passion for souls,
Oh, for a pity that yearns,
Oh, for a love that loves unto death,
Oh, for a heart that burns.

13

Come on and celebrate!

'To him who is able to keep you from falling and to present you before his glorious presence without fault and with great joy – to the only God our Saviour be glory, majesty, power and authority, through Jesus Christ our Lord, before all ages, now and for evermore! Amen.'

verses 24, 25

A crescendo of praise

The theme of these closing verses is the exciting and joyful news that God is able. Gloriously able! It is a fitting climax to the epistle for Jude focuses our hearts and minds on the greatness of God in the person of Jesus Christ. The living God becomes the theme of our worship and adoration as we grow in our appreciation of his attributes and intrinsic qualities.

In most of his letter, Jude addressed his readers in the third person. As he draws his tiny epistle to a close, Jude changes tack when he speaks in the second person as if to get up close and personal with us.

The various congregations may have felt downtrodden because these synthetic saints had virtually walked all over them. But that was not the end. There was something beyond, something a million times better. One day it would be glory. He wants to assure us that we can make it! We are secure in this life and we are secure in the next life. In a few words, Jude shows us how we move from where we are to where God wants us to be!

Christianity is the only religion that guarantees a happy ending.

Great words about a great God

Jude's last words are one of the finest benedictions ever pronounced in the word of God. It must rank alongside some of the greatest doxologies ever expressed by man. It is a paean of praise as we are lifted higher and higher into the majestic presence of our God. It transcends the ordinary. It surpasses that which is transient and superficial. It reaches into the realm of the sublime. It is magnificent.

It is a celebration of the character of God.

Jude zooms in on the sovereignty of God in the life of the real believer. He talks about the Lord's amazing ability to do what we are unable to do for ourselves. The good news is that it is not confined to the yesterdays of life, nor is it reserved for all our tomorrows. It is in the present tense which means we benefit from it today. He is the God who has done it before, he is the God who can do it again.

Power for life

God's power is measureless and limitless. In his omnipotence, there is nothing which he cannot do. He is the God of miracles. He is the God who specialises in performing feats of incredible magnitude. He is the God of the humanly impossible.

He *'will keep you from falling'*. What a beautiful hope that is! What a profound sense of security that should plant in our hearts. To know that the Lord will keep us in the best and worst of times, that is all we need to know. The apostates blew it big time, they had fallen off their pedestal, they made a real shambles of life, their lives were an absolute mess. But, says Jude, the real believer will be kept from falling.

We cannot fall *from* grace. That is a misnomer. We fall *into* grace!

And so, day by day, the nail scarred hand of the Lord is upon us for good. Jude's reassurance is that God will guard us so that we are exempt from stumbling and never trip or make a false step. As Christopher Green points out, 'We will never fall over our own feet, nor will someone else be able to wrong-foot us!' Our great God is just as able to keep us as he was able to save us in the first place.

An equine example

The idea of God providing a safety net for his people is seen in Jude's turn of phrase. The language he uses is borrowed from the world of horse trials. In the average cross-country circuit, riders jump fences of varying height, they go up and down steep slopes, they go through rivers, and over all kinds of obstacles.

We cringe and hold our breath when a horse stumbles and the rider is thrown. Against all the odds, the skilful rider manages to stay in the saddle and, in so doing, succeeds in keeping his mount from stumbling. Somehow he keeps the horse in balance and guides it in the right way.

Jude is more or less saying that God is able to keep us from falling as if we were a horse and he were the rider. That means, the rider on your back is the Lord Jesus himself!

- He is holding the reins of your life.
- He will guide you.
- He will keep you from falling.
- He will put you on the right track.
- He will bring you safely to heaven.

The word of God

One of the ways that the Lord keeps us from falling is by his word. Perhaps, at this moment, you are facing an alluring temptation or something is really getting on top of you. It is with leaden steps and a heavy heart that you wend your way to church on a Sunday morning.

It is almost as if God drags you there kicking and screaming.

And when you get there, the visiting preacher, who does not know you from Adam or Eve, speaks from the Bible on the very matter that is causing you so much hassle and hurt.

Has that ever happened to you? The chances are, it probably has! It has certainly happened to me. Well, there is only one explanation for it. That is what takes place when God uses his word to keep us from falling.

The Spirit of God

He also keeps us from falling by his Holy Spirit. Have you ever come to a point in your life when you can take no more and you want to call it quits and throw the towel into the ring? You have felt under the weather and you have crashed to your knees before the Lord and all you have been able to say is, 'Lord, aaahhhh!' In all honesty, that was how you felt. The cheering news is that the Lord understands precisely how we feel for he knows what makes us tick.

The amazing thing is that so often in such crisis moments a strength is imparted to us from somewhere, a peace comes upon our heart, a light shines into our mind, the burden is eased, and then it is removed. That is the Holy Spirit of God within you. You see, he is able to keep us from falling.

The providence of God

God also keeps us from falling by his providence. Imagine yourself in the position of someone who is determined that he or she has just about had enough of the Christian faith. You are just about to walk out the front door and slam it in God's face, when the telephone rings or someone sends you a text message on your mobile. On the other end of the line is a Christian friend. Unknown to them, their call has come just when you needed it most! It hits you between the eyes that people do care, after all.

That unexpected and unscheduled *tête-à-tête* changes the landscape. The fact is, if it had been five minutes later, you would have been down the town with a huge chip on your shoulder against the Lord. But in the providence of a loving God, the timing could not have been better, it was spot-on and perfect.

Not a coincidence, more like a God-incidence!

No matter how we look at it, that is yet another token that the Lord is on our side. The truth is, he wants us to follow him no matter what the circumstances might be.

The angels of God

He also keeps us from falling by deploying his angels on our behalf. I think this is particularly relevant to our study because Jude has spoken many times about angels and their unique ministry. We know from Scripture that angels are 'ministering spirits sent to serve those who will inherit salvation' (Hebrews 1:14). In other words, like a guardian, they watch over us and God uses them to fulfil his purpose in the grand scheme of things.

In our lives, the Lord keeps his eye on the big picture!

The fatherly nature of God

It may sound like a contradiction but there are times, in his sovereign wisdom, when God keeps us from falling by letting us fall. I think the classic example is that of the apostle Peter. Do you remember his vehement protests on the night that Jesus was betrayed? There he was, with his pride, his self-reliance, his arrogance; all of that needed to be broken otherwise he would make shipwreck of his Christian faith.

To combat this, what did the Lord do? He allowed Peter to fall.

A rerun of the narrative goes like this:

- Christ was arrested.
- Peter followed at a safe distance.
- They were in the courtyard.
- Within minutes, some of the locals came up to Peter and challenged him about his association with Jesus.
- Peter was gobsmacked, he was scared stiff.
- He opened his mouth and protested his innocence.

While the drama was unfolding in Peter's life, Jesus was just across the courtyard, on trial. The Lord turned and looked straight at Peter. At that psychological moment, the big burly fisherman wished the ground would open for he remembered the words the Lord had spoken to him a little while earlier. The Bible tells us that Peter 'went out and wept bitterly' (Luke 22:62). The poor guy was devastated, he was broken by the experience.

Peter was allowed to fall, but the taste of it was so unpalatable and hard to swallow that, as far as we know, he never denied the Lord Jesus again. For him, it was a lesson learned the hard way! In his goodness and grace, the Lord accepted him back and gave him a fresh commission. We know from scouring the annals of church history that there came a point when Peter was prepared to die for his Lord.

It was such a bitter thing for Peter when the Lord looked him straight in the eye that it melted Peter's heart. The lesson is that our God is able to keep us from falling by allowing us to fall, even for a fleeting moment.

The divine agenda

That is the principal reason why Jude is praising him here! Because God is able to keep us. He really is! And he will continue to keep us, by his stupendous power, until we come to the end of life's journey. The question is, when we reach the end of the road, what will he do?

Well, Jude says, he will *'present you before his glorious presence without fault and with great joy'*. It really is quite exciting when we think of the fantastic programme that God has mapped out for each one of his redeemed children.

After the trumpet sounds, when the Lord comes to the air for his people, and we are ushered into his immediate presence, we will stand before him at the judgment seat of Christ. The Bema is spoken of in 2 Corinthians 5:10 as the place of assessment for real believers. It is the hour of appraisal, the moment of examination, for the servants of God.

Here comes the bride

After the hour of grand review has passed, our Lord then presents his beautiful bride at the court of heaven. He does it with enormous pleasure and satisfaction. This is the thought encapsulated in the heart of Paul and often transposed in his writings to various churches (*cf.* 2 Corinthians 11:2; Ephesians 5:27; Colossians 1:21, 22).

Think of it: we will be there, radiant and without fault, but he is the one who steals the show! Standing by his side, we will be clothed in the white linen garment of his impeccable righteousness. Perfected, we will be his pride and joy, forever.

To quote C S Lewis, 'This God is going to take the feeblest and the filthiest of us and turn us into dazzling, radiant, immortal creatures pulsating with all the energy and joy and wisdom and love that we could possibly imagine. He is going to turn us into bright stainless mirrors that reflect back his character perfectly.'

Basically, Jude is wanting to assure them, if the Lord can do that at some date in the future, then it is no problem for him to look after them (and us) in today's world!

Worthy to be praised

Jude proclaims that *'glory, majesty, power and authority'* be directed to God. Christopher Green writes, 'He wants us to respond with praise to a God whose magnificent dominion is unchallengeable for ever.'

I think the choice of words is interesting. Apart from the first word in the ascription of praise, the other words carry the connotation of being subject to God. They are terms which are used in relation to a king or one who rules. This expression of praise is, therefore, an expression of submission to the Lord. It is a proclamation that it is right that God should command us and that all his people should be subordinate to him.

Glory to God

'Glory is doctrine gone emotional.' (Calvin Miller)

It is the great reality of God. It reminds us of the brightness of God. Everywhere God is, is glorious. Everything God does is glorious. Glory is the sum total of all that God is. It is the displayed supremacy of God. It speaks of a concern for the fame and adulation of God. It is the public, visible, and acclaimed presence of God.

* Moses saw it at Mount Sinai.
* It was represented in the shekinah cloud which hovered over the tabernacle and temple.
* Sadly, it departed at the time of the exile (*cf.* Ezekiel 10:18).
* After many years, it was again seen on earth in the face of the Lord Jesus Christ.

The biblical narrative informs us that the apostles were privileged to have 'seen his glory, the glory of the One and Only, who came from the Father, full of grace and truth' (John 1:14). So far as we are concerned, we will see it only when he brings us before his glorious presence in that final day.

Worship the king

- *'Majesty'* gives an unerring sense of the transcendent sovereignty of God. It signifies his eternal right to rule and reign. He is not simply King; he *is* King of kings! He is not simply Lord; he *is* Lord of lords! As G. Campbell Morgan intimates, 'The fixed point in the universe, the unalterable fact, is the throne of God.'
- *'Power'* speaks of the unrivalled strength and force of God. It underlines his unique claim to his throne. Actually, the word it translates, *kratos*, is only ever used of God himself and his work. To ascribe power to him is to rejoice in the fact that all heaven and earth are under his sway and, at the same time, it condemns all who seek to oppose him.
- *'Authority'* is a recognition of his right to use such power. It is the freedom for him to do whatever he desires without hindrance.

There are other nuances in other biblical doxologies. For example, in Revelation 5:12 the innumerable company of heaven sings, 'Worthy is the Lamb'. The word 'worthy' would have been used by the crowd in acclaiming an athlete who had won a vital victory. The praise that is given would, therefore, focus on the remarkable achievement of the one being praised.

In that sense, Jesus has been eminently successful. In the words of Peter Marshall, *'It is better to fail in a cause that will ultimately succeed than to succeed in a cause that will ultimately fail.'* Jesus has won and will win!

This doxology at the end of Jude, however, is slanted more towards the idea that the one being praised should be worshipped through loyal submission to him.

Tying up the loose ends

There are a couple of questions remaining which need to be asked and answered in the light of Jude's benediction.

- When should these sentiments be ascribed to the Lord?
- What is the timescale of his praise?

Jude's answer is almost beyond our comprehension. He takes us back before the beginning of time for he refers to *'before all ages'*. He continues by encouraging us to ascribe glory to the Lord *'now'*. Then he rounds it off by declaring that God is to be worshipped *'for evermore'*.

This threefold reference to past, present, and future is unique in Jewish and early Christian doxologies. Normally there is a reference to the present and the future, that is par for the course. But Jude, with a touch of inspirational genius, refers us back into eternity past and that, it has to be said, is most unusual.

The uniqueness of Jesus

Jude's choice of words is probably another way of subtly underlining the pre-eminence of the Lord Jesus Christ. The false teachers who had wormed their way into the early church denied him as the only Sovereign and Lord (*cf.* verse 4). But Jude, in a deft touch, turns our attention to the praise of God and, in so doing, astutely raises the question of how God was praised in the epochs before time began.

Oh yes, there were angels in heaven, but the Scriptures plainly state that they are not eternal beings. They were created. Before they arrived on the scene, how was God praised? Jude tells us that he was and it came from within the unity of the Trinity.

Here is the uniqueness of the Lord Jesus Christ.

John Benton affirms that *'he is eternally one with the Father, and eternally the one through whom glory is brought to the Father.'*

There is no-one, angelic or human, who can compare with him. And so, once again, Jude pulls the carpet from under the feet of the false teachers. In a sentence, their foolish pretensions are punctured.

We can see what Jude has done! He spins us back before the creation of the universe and says that God had this unimaginable power *'before all ages'*. Despite the apparent godlessness of today's world, he retains it right *'now'*. And nothing and no-one will replace him *'for evermore'*.

Good enough for David

It seems to me that Jude is merely echoing the exuberant praise of David when he said, 'Praise be to you, O Lord, God of our father Israel, from everlasting to everlasting. Yours, O Lord, is the greatness and the power and the glory and the majesty and the splendour, for everything in heaven and earth is yours. Yours, O Lord, is the kingdom; you are exalted as head over all. Wealth and honour come from you; you are the ruler of all things. In your hands are strength and power to exalt and give strength to all. Now, our God, we give you thanks, and praise your glorious name' (1 Chronicles 29:10-13).

God on our team

This is where the rubber hits the road. This is where the doxology is rooted in the reality of everyday living. When we take it all together and note that ascribed unto him are *'glory, majesty, power and authority'* – all these combine to remind us that our God is omnipotent, omnipresent, and omniscient.

- God is all-strong,
- God is all-seeing, and
- God is present in all situations.

Even theirs! And when we think of it, yours and mine as well!

Lost for words

This is the great God with whom we have to do. The fact is, when we have tried our best to say something about Jude's four words, we have no option but to admit our failure adequately to define or explain them. Such moments tend to reveal the poverty of human language.

When we read a benediction like this, our eyes catch a vision of one who is glorious in his brightness and we gladly pay him the homage of our humbled hearts. We look beyond our puny selves to the unutterable regal being of the one who sits upon the throne and we crown him king in our lives. We fix our gaze upon one who is limitless in the extent of his rule and, in response, we bow our hearts and submit to his control over all that we seek to do. Confronted with our weakness, we behold the unlimited strength of his might and are comforted with the assuring words that we can do all things through Christ who is our strength.

No time restrictions in eternity

When faced with such an encounter, Jude can write no more! He tries to encompass eternity within the poor limits of human vocabulary and, in so doing, supplies us with one of the most incredible utterances ever penned upon such a subject. And then, Jude closes his inspired epistle with the words, *'before all time, now, and for evermore'*. What a way to bring it to a fitting finale!

Before the stars were set in their proper courses to mark off time, throughout all the aeons which have been recorded in heaven since time began, and on into the measureless future of God's unfolding purposes, these four divine attributes have belonged, do belong, and will forever belong to God.

Eternally, he is God! In time, he is the 'now' God!

Amen!

In the wonder of the contemplation of such fantastic truths, the quill of the inspired apostle is laid down, his lips become dumb. What more can he say? What a fantastic way to end a letter. It really is breathtaking. It is enough to blow the mind.

'Amen' – one word that says all that needs to be said. It means, 'what I have written is true, these are faithful words'.

Every true believer will want to echo the last word of the last epistle of the New Testament. We join hands with Jude in saying a hearty *'amen'* because all has been said. However, there is a real sense in which all has not been done!

We need to support his *'amen'* with actions and attitudes suited to the solemn revelations which God has given us to warn and instruct us in the dark days which are ahead before the great apostasy has run its course.

Facing the future

With the word of God in our hearts and the Bible in our hands, we step out into an unknown tomorrow with the certainty that one day the last step will be taken and we will be with the Lord whom we dearly love.

Over there, we will meet up and together we will have the pleasure of happy fellowship with our friend Jude. We will be able to sit and talk of the many priceless jewels we mined when reflecting upon his timely letter.

And best of all,

> *When by the gift of his infinite grace,*
> *I am afforded in heaven a place,*
> *Just to be there and to look on his face,*
> *Will through the ages be glory for me.*

Study Guide

~ compiled by John White ~

Read through the entire epistle of Jude – preferably two or three times at a single sitting – and, before answering the questions below, note down the things you think make its message specially relevant for today.

Verse 1

1. Some folk referred to Jude as 'the Lord's brother' (*cf.* 1 Corinthians 9:5), but Jude calls himself *'a servant of Jesus Christ and a brother of James'*. What impression does that leave on your mind as to the kind of person Jude was?

2. What is the threefold description of Christians in this verse? Explain in your own words what each phrase means, and how do these truths make you feel?

3. When thinking about these three facets of Christian experience, why does Jude hark back to the Old Testament?

Verse 2

4. What does our need for *'mercy ... in abundance'* tell us about ourselves, our situation, and our God?

5. Are you experiencing *'peace'* on a day by day basis? If not, what do you think has driven it away, and how can you get it back?

6. Why does receiving *'mercy'* and knowing *'peace'* result in us having a *'love'* for others?

Verse 3

7. What is your understanding of the word *'salvation'* and how does that link in to your personal relationship with Jesus Christ?

8. What key insights does Jude give us into what ought to be a pastor's role towards those in his care?

9. Jude refers to *'the faith'* in this verse, what does he specifically mean by it? How can your church, and you as an individual, *'contend'* for it? Why is it important to do this?

10. How can something which was given *'once for all'* nearly 2,000 years ago be relevant for life in today's world? Does this mean that Christianity must always be old fashioned? If not, why not?

11. *'Saints!'* How do you feel when applying that label to yourself?

Verse 4

12. What safeguards can we put in place to ensure that individuals who would harm the church do not *'slip in among'* us?

13. In what ways are you tempted to use God's grace as an excuse for doing wrong? How can you avoid this?

14. Jude often uses the words *'godless'* or *'ungodly'* in the course of his comments (*cf.* verses 15, 18). Putting these three verses together, what did Jude understand as ungodliness?

15. What does it mean to *'deny Jesus Christ'*? Are we guilty as individuals or, perhaps, corporately as a church, of this mindset?

Verses 5-7

16. As well as Jude, Paul, Peter, and John, were keen to urge their readers to remember what they already knew, and to learn from it (*cf.* 2 Timothy 2:8, 14; 2 Peter 1:12; 1 John 2:20, 21). How can we get the most out of what we already know and, at the same time, make sure we do not forget it in the future?

17. What were the separate failings of each of the three groups in these verses that caused their destruction? Can you think of situations today where these warnings are particularly relevant and need to be listened to?

18. Do you think the warnings in these verses apply to true Christians, or to those who only appear to be Christians? Either way, what does it mean that they will be *'destroyed'*? [The illustration that Jude uses in verse 5 is also used by Paul in 1 Corinthians 10:1-13; it might help if you read that passage too.]

Verses 8-11

19. A recurring theme in the book of Jude has to do with respecting authority (*cf.* verses 6, 8-11). What do these verses tell us about how we should, (a) respond to authority, and, (b) exercise authority in church, home, and society?

20. Why does the archangel Michael have the attitude that he does towards the devil? What is the lesson here for us when speaking and thinking about *'celestial beings'*?

21. What were the specific failings of Cain (*cf.* Genesis 4:1-15), Balaam (*cf.* Numbers 22-25, 31:8, 16), and Korah (*cf.* Numbers 16:1-35)? How might these failings be reflected in today's church?

Verses 12-16

22. The word *'blemishes'* (NIV) might also mean 'hidden rocks'. The verse would then read, 'these men endanger your love feasts'. What dangers do such shepherds 'who feed only themselves' bring to the church and, consequently, to themselves (*cf.* Ezekiel 34:8-10)?

23. Billowy clouds and leafy trees look good, but fancy displays without fruitful deeds are useless! What are some of the ways you might slip into this kind of self-deception? How does this help us to assess the true worth of our work for God?

24. Enoch's 'second coming' prophecy is not in the biblical record. To some folk that is an extremely serious problem, how may it be resolved?

25. A lot is said about the judgment of God in verses 14 and 15. What is the difference, if any, in this context, between an act of revenge and an act of retribution?

Verses 17-19

26. What does it mean that we are said to be living in the *'last times'*? When does this specific era begin and end? What makes it different from other 'times' that are alluded to in Scripture?

27. The *'scoffers'* here are not men and women outside the church, but those who are inside the church. Who are they scoffing at, and why? Can you think of any modern parallels?

28. *'These are the men who divide you'.* Have you ever experienced the pain and trauma of a church split? What lessons have you learned from that distressing experience?

Verse 20

29. In what ways do you think it is appropriate to call the Christian faith *'most holy'*? How can we *'build ourselves up'* in it?

30. Is doctrine important for the Christian? If so, why?

31. Someone has said that 'real religion means realising we depend on God for everything, and prayer is the expression of that dependence.' How can this type of thinking help us to pray? And how does it also help to remember, as Jude says, that we can *'pray in the Holy Spirit'*?

Verse 21

32. *'Keep yourselves in God's love,'* says Jude. How?

33. What is the right balance that needs to be struck between *'keeping'* and *'waiting'*, in other words, between activity in this world and the keen anticipation of life in the next?

34. Choose a couple of the following and carefully think through how this balance might apply to your chosen scenarios: buying and furnishing a house; engaging in leisure pursuits; work and its related stresses; being a good neighbour; involvement in local and/or national politics; campaigning for the environment and 'green' issues; helping the poor and those who are marginalised to the fringe of society.

35. How does the exhortation for us to *'keep ourselves in God's love'* sit comfortably alongside Jude's comment in verse 1 where he indicates that we are *'loved by God and kept by Jesus Christ'*?

Verses 22, 23

36. These verses see the church as a kind of 'rescue' service, bringing back those who have wandered away from Christ and the faith. What approaches and attitudes are advocated by Jude as we try to rescue those who are slipping away?

37. Are there individuals who are beyond the reach of God's grace?

Verses 24, 25

38. The phrase *'him who is able'* which Jude employs is also mentioned in Romans 16:25, Ephesians 3:20 and 2 Corinthians 9:8. What do these verses together tell us about God's care of us and his commitment to us?

39. Jude uses a different word for *'keep'* in this verse when compared with the word he used earlier in verse 21. In that verse, it means 'keep alert and active'; in this verse, it means 'guard' or 'protect' like a sentry or shepherd (the same basic word is used in Luke 2:8 where the shepherds keep watch over their sheep, and in Acts 12:4 where the soldiers guard Peter). What do you think are some of the ways in which God stands guard over our lives? How can we best cooperate with him in this?

40. Jesus was *'without fault'* (*cf.* 1 Peter 1:19). What is the link between his purity and ours? How does one guarantee the other?

Jude ends his letter with a note of joy and praise, and so should we! Meditate for a few moments on our glorious future (verse 24) and our glorious God (verse 25), and spend some quality time in praising *'the only God our Saviour'*. Amen!